Principles Worth Protecting

Christian Education Ministry Group
Cooperative Baptist Fellowship

Principles
Worth
Protecting

Gary E. Parker

Smyth & Helwys Publishing, Inc.
Macon, Georgia

ISBN   1-880837-18-8

Principles Worth Protecting
by Gary E. Parker

Copyright © 1993
Smyth & Helwys Publishing, Inc.
Macon, Georgia

Printed in the United States of America.

The paper used in this publication meets the minimum
requirements of American Standard for Information
Sciences—Permanence of paper for Printed Library Materials,
ANSI Z39.48–1984.

Library of Congress Cataloging-in-Publication Data

Parker, Gary E.
Principles worth protecting / Gary E. Parker.
vi + 88 pp.   6x9" (15x23 cm.)
ISBN 1-880837-18-8 (alk. paper)
1. Baptists—Doctrines. I. Title.
BX6331.2.P27 1993
286'.1—dc20   93-14911
                                                    CIP

Contents

This book is dedicated
to the late Dr. John Carlton,
former Professor of Preaching
at Southeastern Baptist Theological Seminary

He taught me that principles
are worth the price
they always demand.

Acknowledgments

This book first came into being as a series of messages delivered at the First Baptist Church of Jefferson City, Missouri. Though not everyone there agreed with all of the conclusions reached in these messages, the congregation believed in the freedom of the pulpit and so accepted the right of their pastor to preach them. For that, I give thanks.

I also give thanks to those individuals who read particular chapters and clarified my thinking and my understanding of Baptist history and thought.

I express appreciation to Mrs. Judy Warson, my faithful secretary who typed and printed and typed some more. Her steadfast efforts made this and other work possible.

Finally, I salute the Baptists of every generation who remained fixed to principles and refused to yield them for the sake of personal safety and institutional sanction. They are the real heroes.

Chapter One

The Rock Beneath Us: A Principled People

Exodus 17:8-13

A Man and A Baby

Four years ago, while flying from Nashville, Tennessee, to Charlotte, North Carolina, I noticed a man in his mid-thirties sitting one row up and one aisle over from me on the plane. A new father myself at the time, I noticed this man because he held an infant boy in his arms. I watched with interest as the man talked to his child, as he patted him, and as he showed him off to the woman sitting beside him. After we were airborne, the father settled into the routine of the flight. He pushed his seat back, tucked the baby into his shoulder, and closed his eyes. All seemed well. I turned my attention to the book I was reading.

About thirty minutes later, I paused for a moment and looked over again at my flying companions. The man had fallen asleep. His head tilted to the side, and his mouth gaped open. He breathed deeply and regularly. His arms rested slack at his sides. All seemed well—except for one thing. The baby boy had slipped down into the man's lap and was about to roll off his knees into the aisle of the plane. If someone didn't wake up the father, he was going to drop the baby!

The Children in Danger

When I think of Baptist principles today, this image filters through my mind and haunts me. It haunts me because Southern

Baptists have historically cherished a number of theological "babies," birthed to us by our scriptures and our history. We have held a number of beloved principles close to our hearts and called them our children.

In his *Axioms of Religion*, Dr. E. Y. Mullins, known by Baptists as an historical giant in education and theology, spoke of the value of Baptist principles. He said, "God has given to the Baptists of the world a great and sublime task in *the promulgation of principles* on the preservation of which the spiritual and political hopes of the world depend."[1]

Mullins was right! God gave us certain principles that remain vital to us and, through us, remain crucial to the world.

In times past we Baptists showed our pride in these children by claiming them as honored parts of our Baptist family. We introduced our principles to our Christian and non-Christian brothers and sisters. We clutched them to our shoulders and protected them as any proud parent would. If we could have, we would have taken pictures of our principles and showed them off to our friends and neighbors.

Now, however, our children face genuine danger. They face the danger of living in a house controlled by new parents. Some of the new parents love other principles more than the old ones. In some cases, the parents actually despise the children they were bequeathed. As a result, our principles face threats to their survival. They face some enemies who intentionally want to orphan them. They face other dangers from those who don't specifically want to harm them but who won't do anything to help either. To protect Baptist principles, we need to identify the dangers to them. The danger to our principles arises from three sources.

Only the Strong Survive

First, *we face the danger of someone pulling our children from our arms.* Our principles will face threats from other people who don't agree with what we believe and want to distort or destroy it. Inevitably, a person or a group that stands for something will end up in conflict with one who believes in an opposite principle.

Every principle any of us holds will find opposition from enemies who live by differing concepts.

For example, a capitalist and a communist will struggle over the best way to maintain a just economic system. A Republican and a Democrat will disagree over what to do to solve the problems of the inner city. A fundamentalist Christian and a liberal Christian will contest the proper relationship between church and state. The beliefs that support your life will always meet opponents who want to defeat and supplant those underpinnings.

The opponents won't always act with hostility in the battle over principle. Indeed, as Americans we've always believed in the free "market place of ideas," the arena of academic and lay discussion in which people seek to persuade others to a new way of thought. In these struggles it's always possible for one person to convert the other.

It is also possible for one person (or system) to defeat the other so conclusively in argument, at the polls, or militarily that either the defeated party loses faith in what it believes or the victorious party oppresses the beliefs of those defeated. In these instances, the rhetoric increases, the anger intensifies, and the victor uses the triumph as an excuse and an opportunity to eradicate previously held principles.

For the Sake of Peace

The head-on confrontation between two people or two systems of principle doesn't frighten me nearly so much as the second threat. In fact, the head-on confrontation almost never changes anyone's beliefs. Two strong people will either agree to disagree or go their separate ways.

The worst tragedy occurs when a strong system (or person) meets a weak system (or person). When this happens, the person of shaky or untested principle faces the temptation to yield the floor in the interest of peace. So, the principles they once cherished disappear.

Our children face the danger of parents who give them up in order to avoid a conflict. Tragically, this occurs far too often in Southern

Baptist life (and in life in general for that matter). In the heat of
conflict, the weaker person drops an important principle.

Whether we like it or not, principles do require defense. To
defend implies conflict between two opposing views. When Patrick
Henry uttered his famous words, "Give me liberty or give me
death," he exhibited this truth. Principle will bring confrontation.
When confrontation comes, we make one of two choices. We stand
for what we believe or we yield to another in order to maintain
peace. Unfortunately, we maintain peace at too high a price. We
maintain peace at the price of principle.

The scriptures depict Jesus as a man of peace. Indeed, the
angels declared his birth as an opportunity for "peace among
men." Yet, the Prince of Peace never claimed we should seek peace
at any price. Instead, on one occasion, Jesus said, "Do not think
that I came to bring peace on the earth; I did not come to bring
peace, but a sword (Matt 10:34)." Then, he proved what he said
about himself on more than one occasion. He fought Pharisaism on
every hand. He stood up for justice and equality. He spoke out
against hypocrisy and showy religion and pride and prejudice.

Jesus faced conflict every day of his public ministry precisely
because he lived a life of principle. Ultimately, principle carried
Jesus to a dusty hill, nailed him to a Roman tree, and pulled the
last breath from his lips. Jesus died for people and for principle.
He refused to crucify principle on the gibbet of peace.

In meeting after meeting at the state, associational, and national
level, you're likely to hear a refrain similar to this, "In the interest
of harmony," or "In order to keep our unity," or "So we can stay
at peace. "When you hear such words, two things might be
happening. First, the person speaking might genuinely believe the
issue is unimportant and shouldn't be a point of division. Or,
second, the person might be using the appeal to peace as a way to
close debate over an important principle. In the search for peace
we often decimate, distort, or ignore our foundational beliefs.
Under the banner of "unity" and harmony" people will often give
up what they thought they believed.

What's In It For Me?

Baptist principles face one more danger. This monster looms as the most frightening of all. *People will give up principle to protect or advance themselves.* In his play, *A Man for All Seasons*, Robert Bolt wrote, "We speak of being anchored to our principles. But if the weather turns nasty, you up with an anchor and let it down where there's less wind, and the fishing's better."[2]

Though most of us would like to say Bolt has it all wrong, in our more honest moments, we admit he has written the truth. We often claim a principle until it threatens to cost us something. Then, when we see the threat, we often abandon the principle.

I remember an old joke from my childhood. The Lone Ranger and Tonto found themselves in a battle against 50 fierce Indians. Gunfire blazed, and an arrow hit the Lone Ranger in his leg. He lamented to Tonto. "Well, it looks like we're not going to make it. I think we're going to die. "Tonto looked back at his former friend and said, "Whatdaya mean *we*, white man?"

We face the temptation that Tonto faced. When trouble comes, we want to bail out and find a place of safety for ourselves.

Yet, if we're not willing to pay a price for our principles, we can't really claim them as ours. A principle without a price has no power. If you won't risk losing something for a belief, then it's not a conviction, it's a convenience!

The dictionary defines principle as "a comprehensive and fundamental law, doctrine, or assumption; a rule or code of conduct; a habitual devotion to right principles; an underlying faculty or endowment."[3]

Within this definition I hear one basic truth: A principle serves as an underpinning, as a foundation stone, as a pivot point for life. Without principle the person and the group (of whatever nature) exists like a spineless jellyfish, with no backbone to give it courage. In popular jargon, a person without principle, one who "stands for nothing," will "fall for everything."

Historically, Baptists have "stood for something. "Now, though, it seems we're forgetting our principles, we're falling

asleep with our children, we're giving them up to those who deny
or distort the value of what we once cherished.

A Biblical Image

In Exodus 17:8-13 we see the people of Israel in battle against the
Amalekites. Moses sent Joshua and a contingent of troops to
engage the enemy. He took Aaron and Hur with him to the top of
a hill to watch and pray. As the battle raged, Moses raised his
arms into the air. The soldiers fighting below saw his strength, and
his strength inspired theirs so that they fought with renewed vig-
or. The battle swayed in their favor.

Then Moses' arms grew weary. He dropped them to rest. The
men in the trenches saw his fatigue, and they were weary, too.
Their zeal lagged, and the battle turned against them.

Aaron saw what he needed to do. He picked up a stone and
placed it under Moses to support him. Then, he placed Hur on one
side of Moses, and he stood on the other. Together, they lifted the
arms of their leader high toward the clouds.

Joshua's men saw Moses' renewed energy. They took heart
again and slashed their way to victory over the enemy.

I don't know what message this image brings to you. It brings
this word to me. Baptists today find themselves in all kinds of
struggles. We struggle against evil from outside the body of Christ.
We fight to defend the faith against those hostile to it and those
indifferent to it. Sadly, we also struggle within the body of Christ.
We seek to define the type of faith we'll enjoy and the style of life
our people will lead.

In the midst of our struggles, we need a "stone" on which to
stand. We require supports to hold us up. We find our foundation
stones in the principles we hold dear. Without these principles we
cannot overcome the struggles of our faith. With them, we can
defeat any enemy before us.

In the pages that follow, we will consider eight Baptist principles: the priesthood of the believer, the authority of scripture, the
autonomy of the local church, no Lord but Christ, no creed but the
Bible, the separation of Church and state, the right of dissent, ser-

vant leadership, and unity within diversity, These principles have acted as the glue holding the corporate body together. So, they deserve our attention.

A Man of Principle

In sixteenth-century England two men of iron will clashed. In the beginning, the two men were friends. Henry VIII, the King of England, knighted Thomas More in 1521 and appointed him the Lord Chancellor of London in 1529.

Sadly, though, the two men found themselves at odds. More refused to acknowledge Henry's divorce from Katharine of Aragon as legitimate. He also refused to subscribe to Henry's Act of Supremacy, which established Henry as superior to the Catholic pope and made him head of the Church of England.

Unable to silence More, Henry had him thrown into prison in 1534. He asked him to recant. More refused, more than once. Finally, the king ordered his former friend's execution. The guards beheaded him.

According to the accounts, More maintained his composure to the end. His final words were, "I die the king's good servant, but God's first."[4]

History remembers More as a man of principle. Let's hope history continues to remember Baptists as a people of principle as well.

Notes

[1]E. Y. Mullins, *Axioms of Religion*, as cited by Henry Cook, *What Baptists Stand For* (London: The Carey Kingsgate Press, 1947) 9.

[2]*The New International Thesaurus of Quotations* (New York: Thomas Howell, 1970) 505.

[3]*Webster's New Collegiate Dictionary* (Springfield, MA: G. and C. Merriam Company, 1979) 908.

[4]Richard Marius, *Thomas More: A Biography* (New York: Alfred A. Knopf, 1984) 514.

Chapter Two

Our Firstborn Child: Priesthood of the Believer

Luke 23:44-45

Images of Priesthood

I walked into the hospital room without advance notice. I hadn't called, and I didn't knock since the door was open. Instantly, I stopped. The man was on his knees. His gown gaped open in the back. His hands were interlocked in front of his chest. His head was bowed, and his eyes were closed. He was in prayer.

One Sunday night, I called the church I pastored into business conference to debate whether or not we ought to buy a new van. Our youth and their parents were enthusiastic about the purchase. A few of our fiscal conservatives weren't. The debate flowed back and forth. Finally, we voted. The "for the van" group won with 82 per cent of the vote.

Bob came to see me on Tuesday morning. He had a "bone to pick with me," he said. I asked, "What's the trouble?" Bob said, "Pastor, I don't like this drama we've been using in worship. It doesn't do a thing for me and most of the older people. I just wanted you to know I don't think we ought to do it anymore."

The room at the nursing home was too hot for me, but Ethel had a blanket over her legs. A Bible lay on top of her blanket, opened to Hebrews 10. She was certain she had lost her salvation because of a sin she had once committed. I tried to comfort her, to offer an understanding of the text that disturbed her so. She wouldn't accept my explanation. It was my fourth visit with her in the past year, and we had discussed the same text on each visit.

In each of these instances (and each of us could visualize scores of others), I participated in a worthy drama. I watched, I listened, and I shared moments in which people practiced their priesthood. All the persons I have described took seriously their responsibility to practice their Christian belief in their own unique way.

The History of Baptist Priesthood

The phrase "priesthood of the believer" has a long and distinguished history among Baptists. E. Y. Mullins, the early twentieth-century shaper of Southern Baptist theology, said, "This conception of the competency of the soul under God . . . sets forth the distinctive contribution of Baptists to the religious thought of the race."[1]

In *The Baptist Faith and Message*, Herschel Hobbs quoted the statement of faith adopted by the convention in San Francisco in 1962: "Baptists emphasize the soul's competency before God, freedom in religion, and the priesthood of the believer."[2] Hobbs himself declared the principle of the priesthood of the believer the "basic belief of Baptists."[3] He wrote, "There are certain basic things generally held by Baptists today as through past years. But, underlying all of them has been the principle of soul competency in religion."[4]

Evidently, the principle of priesthood was our firstborn child. For centuries Baptists have loved the baby, nurtured the baby, and proudly showed off the baby called priesthood.

Priesthood Under Threat

Unfortunately, a new group of parents now sits in the head chairs of the Baptist household. They have other children they want to protect and display. So, to make room for the new ones, they must move out the old ones. These new parents don't love the old children. In fact, some of them want to push them out of the nest. You can tell it by their words when they speak and by the actions they take. The most glaring example of the new attitude that threatens the doctrine of the priesthood of the believer remains the infamous Resolution Number Five that the Southern Baptist Convention approved in 1988. Though resolutions have no binding authority on any church, the symbolic meaning of such a resolution shouldn't be minimized. What begins as a resolution today can easily become a lifestyle tomorrow.

For the benefit of those uninitiated about Resolution Number Five, let me quote it here.

> WHEREAS, None of the five major writing systematic theologians in Southern Baptist history have given more than passing reference to the doctrine of the Priesthood of the Believer in their systematic theologies; and
>
> WHEREAS, The high profile emphasis on the doctrine of the Priesthood of the Believer in Southern Baptist life is a recent historical development; and
>
> WHEREAS, The Priesthood of the Believer is a term which is subject to both misunderstanding and abuse; and
>
> WHEREAS, The doctrine of the Priesthood of the Believer has been used to justify wrongly the attitude that a Christian may believe whatever he so chooses and still be considered a loyal Southern Baptist; and
>
> WHEREAS, The doctrine of the Priesthood of the Believer can be used to justify the undermining of pastoral authority in the local church.
>
> Be it therefore RESOLVED, That the Southern Baptist Convention meeting in San Antonio, Texas, June 14-16, 1988, affirm it beslief in the biblical doctrine of the Priesthood of the Believer (1 Peter 2:9 and Revelation 1:6); and
>
> Be it further RESOLVED, That we affirm that this doctrine in no way gives license to misinterpret, explain away, demythologlze, or extrapolate out elements of the supernatural from the Bible; and
>
> Be it further RESOLVED, That the doctrine of the Priesthood of the Believer in no way contradicts the biblical understanding of the role, responsibility, and authority of the pastor which is seen in the command to the local church in Hebrews 13:17, "Obey your leaders, and submit to them; for they keep watch over your souls, as those who will give an account:" and
>
> Be it finally RESOLVED, That we affirm the truth that elders, or pastors, are called of God to lead the local church (Acts 20:28).

Obviously, this resolution seeks to do two things. First, it seeks to *undermine* the doctrine of every person's priesthood. Second, it seeks to *undergird* the doctrine of pastoral authority. Those who want to elevate the authority of the pastor over the layperson necessarily need to denigrate one to accomplish the other. It's tough for the dictatorial pastor who wants to proclaim "thus saith the Lord" over every opinion he holds, to combat a layperson who declares, "The Lord told me something different." An open Bible in the hands of every person scares the wits out of those who want a closed mind in their heads instead.

The way the new leadership states it leaves no doubt of their intention. The resolution deliberately attacks the long-cherished child of our faith that we call "priesthood of the believer."

I could give other examples, but perhaps this will suffice to make the point. In our new era of "pastoral popehood" the baby called priesthood faces rejection.

A Definition of Priesthood

I realize not everyone understands what I mean when I write of this priesthood. Maybe you're new to the Baptist family and want me to describe this child to you. Or, you've been in the Baptist household so long you've taken your firstborn for granted and pay little attention to it now. In either case, let me offer an explanation of the meaning of the term.

When I write of this baby called "Priesthood" I can point proudly to his characteristics. I want you to know first, that the Bible gave birth to this doctrine. This is no illegitimate offspring!

From early Jewish history we hear God making a concrete promise to his children. In Exodus 19:6 God asserts: "You shall be to me a kingdom of priests and a holy nation." Speaking to scattered Christians who needed a reminder of their position before God, Peter encouraged them, saying, "You are a holy priesthood . . . acceptable to God through Jesus Christ (1 Pet 2:9)."

Speaking to Timothy, his son in the ministry, Paul wrote, "There is one God, and one mediator between God and men, the man Christ Jesus (1 Tim 2:5)."

Speaking to the future of the Christian believer as God initiates his glorious reign of eternity, John said, "They shall be priests of God and of Christ (Rev 20:6)."

From these texts and others like them, we uncover three implications for the Christian life. First, the priesthood of the believer means each individual person has direct access to God without another person's intervention. We have access in our prayers and in our faith. We can receive a word, an interpretation, a decision from the Lord as easily as anyone else. We require no pope, no confessor, no saint of the church, and no president of a convention to guide us into God's presence.

Second, it means you're responsible for yourself—for your salvation, your ethic, and your life-style. I can't provide for your salvation, and I'm not responsible for your decisions. Certainly, the church supports, teaches, and prays for each believer. But, ultimately no one can coerce you into any particular stripe of morality or theology.

Third, it means each of us has the privilege but also bears the pressure of opening the Bible, reading it, and reaching our decisions about what it means as the power of the Holy Spirit gives us direction.

Instead of relying upon one particular high priest who alone has the right to enter behind the veil to speak with God, the people of faith experience the freedom of pulling aside the veil for themselves.

A Biblical Revelation

In Luke 23:44-45 the scripture describes a dramatic event: "It was now about the sixth hour, and darkness came over the whole land until the ninth hour, for the sun stopped shining. And the curtain of the temple was torn in two." For those knowledgeable of Jewish tradition, this text offers profound symbolism. The curtain in the temple separated people from the Holy of Holies, the inner sanctum of worship. The people outside the sanctum were divided according to their race or gender. The Gentiles were the farthest away from the Holy of Holies (and by implication the furthest away from God). The women were next, in the Court of Women. The almost-inner-circle included the males of Israel and the final group was the priests. But even the priests couldn't go behind the veil. Only one person, the high priest, entered the Holy of Holies, and he went there only once each year, on the Day of Atonement. On that day he carried the sins of the people to the Lord and sacrificed for them so they could receive forgiveness.

The curtain represented a stark reality. The people had to depend upon the high priest to convey their needs to God. They could not approach the Lord on their own.

With the death of Jesus, the separation of the people from God ended. Christ provided direct access to the Father for everybody. The curtain ripped, and with it the Jewish system of human mediation died. Jesus offers the only go-between required. We live as our own priest and can go directly into the throne room of the Lord's grace.

In his book, *Improving Your Serve*, Chuck Swindoll re-tells the story of the "Keeper of the Spring." The town council of an Austrian village in the Alps had hired an old gentleman to keep the debris out of the pools that fed the spring flowing through their town. With faithful regularity, the old man patrolled the hills, removed the leaves and branches, and wiped away the silt. He kept the fresh water flowing. The village became a popular attraction for vacationers. Graceful swans floated in the clear spring, the farmlands were naturally irrigated, and the view from restaurants was picturesque beyond description.

Years passed. One evening the town council met and reviewed the budget. One man asked about the obscure keeper of the spring. He asked, "Who is this old man? Why do we keep him on the payroll? No one ever sees him. For all we know, he's doing us no good." By a unanimous vote, the council dispensed with the old man's services.

For several weeks nothing changed. Then, in early autumn, the trees shed their leaves. Small branches snapped off and fell into the pool. One afternoon someone noticed a yellowish-brown tint in the spring. A couple of days later the water was much darker. Within another week, a slimy film covered sections of the water, and the people smelled a foul odor. The swans and the tourists left. The clammy fingers of disease reached deeply into the village.

Quickly, the embarrassed council called a special meeting. Realizing their gross error, they hired back the old keeper of the spring. Within a few weeks the literal "river of life" began to clear up. The wheels started to turn, and life returned to the hamlet in the Alps once again.

I don't know what you get from this story. I hear this valuable message. Jesus Christ lives as the only sufficient "Keeper of the Springs." He provides the gift of renewal for every believer. We require none other than Christ. To him alone we go for the water of life. No pope, no priest, no council, and no convention serves this function for us. Jesus alone mediates our relationship to God.

Baptists have taken this opportunity seriously and have rejected any practice of any religious group that encourages or teaches the need for any mediator other than Jesus. Baptists have believed the individual has the right to pray directly to God, to debate personal opinions openly and freely, to disagree (even with the pastor's opinions), and to read and interpret the Bible for themselves.

I recognize the danger in such a position. People could become their own individual churches if they took this freedom to the extreme. But, look at the other danger. The other extreme leads to a totalitarian gospel through which one person (the pastor in the local church) or a few people in a national convention dictate to all of us what we must believe and how we must live and worship in order to be acceptable as "good Christians" and "good Baptists." We end up with theology by majority vote rather than theology by individual conscience and scriptural leadership. We have to choose which danger to chance—the danger of individuality or the danger of authoritarianism. Traditionally, Baptists have chosen the first one as the lesser of the two evil possibilities.

Authority Earned, Not Demanded

When I speak of the "priesthood of the believer," I am not denying the necessity of pastoral leadership. That wouldn't be too bright, on my part, would it? After all, I am a pastor. The pastor of a local church deserves respect, attention, and consideration. The church should yield a certain authority to their pastor. My authority, however, comes from what you as a congregation give to me rather than from what I *demand* from you. I have authority by virtue of my call from God. I own authority by virtue of my years of study and preparation. I gain authority by a life-style of service and Christian example to you, my people. But, remember this—there is a difference between authority and authoritarianism.[5]

Jesus spoke specifically to this issue in Mark 10:35-45. Responding to the demands of James and John to give them positions of power in his coming kingdom, Jesus reminded them of the typical worldly practice. "Those who are considered rulers . . . lord it over them and their great ones exercise authority over them." Then Jesus offered the Christian model of leadership: "Whoever desires to be great among you shall be your servant. And whoever of you desires to be first shall be slave of all."

I hear the voices of James and John again in our convention today demanding by a majority vote the right to "lord it over them." Jesus, however, has not changed his opinion to fit the mood of any denominational meeting. He tells us repeatedly, "Whoever desires to be great among you shall be your servant."

The pastor is "called by God to lead the local church," as the resolution of 1988 states, but such leadership does not grant the pastor or a group of pastors of a convention, the right to decree from on high the final word about the direction of the church, the correct interpretation of scripture, or the only position acceptable on social and political issues that come to our attention.

To Lead or To Drive?

Have you ever watched a herd of cattle coming in from the fields for the evening? In my three years in Texas I had the opportunity to watch cattle move. Do you know what I noticed? Cattlemen move their herds in one of two basic ways. Some cattlemen drive their herds with dogs, or with horsemen cracking whips, or, in our modern world, with pickup trucks or helicopters.

Other cattlemen take a second approach. They take a loud, clear bell and hang it around the neck of a faithful cow. Then they get the lead cow moving.

Amazingly, the other cattle hear the call of the clear bell and they *follow* it to the shed.

As a pastor, I want my people to follow my leadership. Sometimes I want them to follow it and they don't. But, I want them to follow it because God has placed the bell of the gospel around my neck and the sound of that bell leads them home to the safety of the shed. I do not want them to follow my leadership because I lash them with the whip of orthodoxy and conformity and pastoral arrogance.

Giving Up the Baby

I said in chapter one that if the father didn't awaken, he would drop the baby. The analogy breaks down a bit here because, in reality, the baby is being wrestled from the father's grip. But he still needs to wake up to fight for his child. The surprising thing to me about this whole situation is that the laypeople of our churches are not fighting more fiercely to protect their family. The irony of any democratic system, the one in which priesthood thrives, is that the people can vote away their freedom. They can vote it away with their ballots in favor of a dictatorship or they can vote it away by the absence of their ballots while the forces of control cast theirs.

When approximately 55 percent of the people of the Southern Baptist Convention lift their hands year after year into the air to vote for the politics of control and against the priesthood of the believer, I ask myself: "Why do they want to vote away their freedom?" Two possible answers came to mind. First, pastors make up the majority of messengers to the convention, and the vote might reflect a pastoral desire to strengthen their own hand. But, I have to admit, thousands of laypeople vote for this anti-priesthood group as well. So, the question remains, "Why?"

I can suggest only one possibility. In a desperate search for certainty in an uncertain age, our people want someone to tell them how to live and what to believe. Out of an insecure need for an authority figure who will direct us in all our thought and action, we give up our freedom. The new parents of our Baptist family pull the child from our arms, and we scarcely put up a whimper.

A Scriptural Call to Freedom

In his letter to the churches in Galatia, the apostle Paul wrote to a group of people confused, as we often are, about the nature of their faith. A segment of believers taught that a person who wanted to trust Christ as Savior must first accept the traditional Jewish rituals. They said that a Christian must first become a Jew. Others, however, denied this need. They believed that a commitment to Jesus Christ was sufficient for salvation. They denied the need for any other doctrine, any other tradition, any other profession.

Paul, under the inspiration of the Holy Spirit sided with this second group. In a ringing exhortation he sounded this battle cry: "Stand fast, therefore, in the liberty by which Christ has made us free, and do not be entangled again with a yoke of bondage (Gal 5:1)."

We need to hear these words again in our convention because a new child called the "Yoke of Bondage" has largely kicked out our first child called "Priesthood of the Believer." But, let me tell you firmly, the "Yoke of Bondage" is an illegitimate child!

"Priesthood" is our first born. We can save the first child only if we stand firm against all efforts to intimidate us, to frighten us, or to silence us. But, if not, he will slip from our grasp to the floor and become a dead corpse of a once-glorious Baptist past.

The Battle Continues

In 1988, in San Antonio, thousands of Southern Baptists visited that city's most famous historical shrine, the Alamo. In that white-stone Spanish mission a brave group of freedom fighters fought to the last man against the numerically superior forces of General Santa Anna of Mexico. We know the outcome of that battle. William Travis, Jim Bowie, Davy Crockett and all the rest lost and died. It appeared Texas would lose its liberty to the oppressors from the South. But, out of the ashes of a burned-out mission-turned-fortress, a new spirit was born. Crying "Remember the Alamo," Sam Houston and his army defeated Santa Anna six weeks later and won freedom from Texas.

Make no mistake about it. We're in a new battle for liberty in Baptist life today. And, liberty has lost battle after battle in the last number of years. But, believing the words of Jesus, "You shall know the truth and the truth shall make you free," we continue to struggle. The struggle may create new forms of fellowship and new channels of ministry among us. After all, priesthood and pastoral popehood don't exist well in the same house.

If we want to keep the child Priesthood, we will need lay-people, the majority of the priests in the Southern Baptist Convention, to join the fray against Bondage. After all, you birthed the child. You protected the child from the beginning. The child needs your help again today. I call upon you to make up your minds and set your hearts now to resist the new parents before the forces of control pull Priesthood irrevocably from our grasp. How you will resist remains to be seen. But, as Baptist priests, we can do no other.

Notes

[1]E. Y. Mullins, *The Axioms of Religion* (Philadelphia: Judson Press, 1908) 50–56.

[2]Hershel H. Hobbs, *The Baptist Faith and Message* (Nashville: Convention Press, 1964) 4.

[3]Ibid., 10.

[4]Ibid., 10.

[5]I will speak in more detail on pastoral authority in Chapter Eight when we consider "servant leadership."

Chapter Three

The God-Breathed Word: The Authority of the Bible

2 Timothy 3:16

My First Bible

I didn't exactly know what to do with it. I had won it in my Sunday school class at the Wesleyan Methodist Church, which I attended (because it was close to my house) as a boy. I didn't win it in a raffle or a bet. Instead, I won it because I had memorized the One Hundredth Psalm. Two sweet-hearted, gray-haired ladies gave Bibles to every fourth grader who memorized one of a number of selected passages.

I took my Bible home and opened it carefully. It was the first one I'd ever owned. I flipped its pages, treating them like valuable jewels. I noticed the big words—Ezekiel, Malachi, Corinthians, Revelation. Some of the words in the section called the New Testament were printed in red. I didn't know it then, but those were the words of Jesus.

I decided to read my Bible. I started the day I brought it home. I finished a few chapters each morning, believing I could read it through by the end of the school year.

Unfortunately, I didn't make it. I did fine with Genesis, and Exodus was okay, too. But Leviticus did me in. I came to a dead end in my Bible reading for the time being. I put the Bible aside.

Over the years, I lost it. To this day, I don't know what happened to the first Bible I ever owned, and that grieves me. Losing my first Bible as a nine-year old, though, grieves me less than the modern "battle for the Bible" that Baptists continue to wage.

When Jesus Christ performed his miracle of redemption in me nine years after I received my first Bible, I came to love and appreciate the value of it. I came to understand, at least in a beginning way, the purpose of the scriptures. I came to view the holy writ as God's communication to me, God's word for my personal spiritual growth. I came to accept the Bible as the authoritative guide to the way I should live.

Unfortunately, within a few years of my salvation experience, I also came to understand another reality— Baptists were struggling among themselves about the way to understand the Bible. In one sense, we're like I was as a nine-year old—we still don't know exactly what to do with the word God has given to us.

In theory, we know full well what to with it. We're to read it, study it, love it, and live it. In reality, though, we ignore it, distort it to fit our own ends, fight over it, and use it for purposes God never intended.

A People of the Book

Baptists have always considered themselves a "people of the Book." Herschel Hobbs wrote, "Baptists believe that the Bible is the inspired written record of God's revelation to men."[1] E. Y. Mullins said, "For Baptists there is one authoritative source of religious truth and knowledge. To that source they look in all matters relating to doctrine, to polity, to the ordinances, to worship and Christian living. That source is the Bible"[2] Russell Dilday, the current president of Southwestern Baptist Theological Seminary, gave his testimony: "One of the primary reasons I am a Southern Baptist is because this denomination has so positively declared its faith in the Bible as the Word of God and the sole authority for faith and practice."[3]

Given our historical allegiance to the scripture, no one should doubt the principle—Baptists believe in the principle of scriptural authority. We believe God inspired the book, God "breathed" it, as 2 Timothy 3:16 reminds us. We don't argue or dispute the truth of inspiration. All Baptists can agree on the principle of biblical authority. Unfortunately, we find ourselves at times in disagreement on the manner or the *method* God used to "breath" it.

For the sake of clarity, let me briefly describe the two methods of inspiration that Baptists have traditionally accepted as valid.

The Dynamic Theory

First, *some Baptists believe in the dynamic theory of inspiration.* This means they believe God worked through the personalities of the writers to give us the message we need to hear. The writers were given freedom under the Holy Spirit to use their perspectives to describe the events. Hobbs described the dynamic theory:

> The Holy Spirit, inspired the thought rather than the exact wording, that the writers were left free to express the truth in their own forms and words, but that in the process the writers were by the spirit guarded from error.[4]

This explains why one of the Gospels doesn't agree in every point with each of the others. Different writers emphasized different aspects of the work and message of Jesus because they heard, saw, and compiled different emphases. The dynamic theory of inspiration accepts the divine *and* the human side of God's work in the world.

The Plenary Verbal View

Second, *some Baptists believe in the plenary verbal theory of inspiration.* This view says that God overcame the individual writers with the power of the Spirit in a way that effectively removed their personalities from the process. The people became recorders of the words given to them by God. Hobbs described the plenary verbal theory: "The Holy Spirit selected the very words of the scriptures and dictated them to the writer."[5] As recorders only, and not creators, the writers could make no mistakes in what they wrote.

Both of these views accept the divine authority of the Bible. As such, they both maintain a high view of scripture and should be acceptable within the Baptist fellowship. As Hobbs said, "Which of these theories one holds has never been a test of orthodoxy among Southern Baptists."[6]

Unfortunately, what Hobbs said has now largely changed. Baptists do find themselves at odds over the method of inspiration of the scriptures. Striving to maintain a high view of scripture, which they saw as under threat, the fundamentalist-conservatives in the Southern Baptist Convention came to insist on the term "inerrancy" to define the Bible revelation. The plenary verbal believers accept this term to describe their stance. They say, "A perfect God could not breath any error. Therefore, the Bible is an inerrant document."

The Original Autographs

Even as our convention leadership insists on the word "inerrancy," however, they make a qualification in their minds. They accept the inerrancy of scripture as it was recorded in what they call "the original autographs." Hobbs wrote,

> This inerrancy, of course, refers to the original manuscripts. Serious students of the Bible know that, through the years, copyists' errors were made. The Holy Spirit does not guard copyists from such any more than he does typesetters.[7]

Since the term "original autograph" is unfamiliar to many people, let me define it briefly. Inerrantists point back to a "perfect manuscript" that, according to this theory, existed in the early decades of the church. Unfortunately, according to this belief, something happened, and we lost the originals. So, even the most ardent inerrantist will admit the Bible we now have has certain unexplainable discrepancies at certain points.

For example, consider the words of W. A. Criswell, longtime leader in the inerrantist camp. He said, "On the original parchment every sentence, word, line, mark, point, pen stroke, jot and tittle were put there by the inspiration of God."[8] Then, in a section dealing with "difficulties" in the Bible, Criswell referred to John 5:4 and said,

> Now this statement regarding the angel disturbing the water seems improbable for many reasons. Upon thorough investigation through textual study we find that the whole thing is the *mistake* of an unknown copyist. Some early scribe, reading John's account, added in the margin his explanation of the healing properties of this intermittent, medicinal spring. A later copyist, thinking that the original scribe had left the text out and had put it in the margin, later embodied this marginal note in the body of the text itself; hence, it came to be handed down and got into our authorized version.[9]

I quoted Criswell at length to make this key point. When a so-called inerrantist preacher holds up his Bible and proclaims "I believe in the inerrant, infallible Word of God," you should recognize that he is making a qualification in his mind that you do not hear. He's saying, "I believe in the inerrant, infallible Word of God as found in the original autographs." Unfortunately, we know of no such autographs from the Bible itself nor from early church history. And, if our perfect God breathed a perfect manuscript for us to have, wouldn't the same perfect God also have managed to keep this perfect manuscript from getting lost? If it was so important for us to have, wouldn't the all-powerful Lord have protected it through the power at his disposal?

It's important for us to embrace the desire of the inerrantist—to keep the doctrine of biblical authority and inspiration at the center of Baptist life. We should, however, ask whether it's necessary to accept the terminology of the inerrantist when the understanding of it includes the necessary qualification of the original autograph.

Emotional and Scholastic Inerrancy

In reality, we face our struggle because we're dealing with what I call an "emotional inerrancy" versus a "scholastic inerrancy." The emotional inerrantist uses the term to denigrate other believers who may love the Lord and the word but use another term to describe it. The emotional inerrantist uses the Bible as a club rather than as a comfort. The emotional inerrantist makes the Bible a place to divide believers rather than as a point to unite the fellowship.

The scholastic inerrantist uses the word much more circum-spectly. In wider evangelical circles, scholars accept the qualifications we have to make with the term. For example, Clark Pinnock, a former professor at New Orleans Baptist Theological Seminary and a god-father to many of the leaders in the inerrancy movement in the Southern Baptist Convention, wrote,

> The category of inerrancy as used today is quite a technical one and difficult to explain exactly. It is postulated of the original texts (auto-graphs) of scripture, not now extant; it is held not to apply to round numbers, grammatical structures, incidental details in texts; it is held to be unfalsifiable except by some indisputable argument.[10]

In other words, though many within Southern Baptist life use the term "inerrancy" to describe the Bible, they do so knowing the Bible contains "difficulties" that the human mind cannot explain. As Criswell said it, the Bible contains "mistakes" that a copyist made that should not be there. Yet, when so-called inerrantist preachers stand up to preach or to decry the liberalism supposedly rampant in our seminaries and mission agencies, the emotional inerrantists act as if the qualifications of the term don't exist.

Out of an admirable desire to maintain a view of scripture as authoritative, at least a few have used the way they describe the Bible as a means to cast suspicion upon the commitment another person has to God and the word God has given to us.

Five Types of Inerrancy

Unfortunately, the inerrancy movement has led to division precisely because of the effort to force everyone to embrace its language, even though the language means different things to different people. In his work, *The Doctrine of the Bible*, David Dockery, the Dean of the School of Theology at The Southern Baptist Theological Seminary, describes five modes of inerrancy.

First, we find "naive inerrancy" (also called the dictation view) that says God dictated "word for word" the text wanted, with almost no involvement by the human writer.

Second, others believe in what Dockery called the "absolute inerrancy" view. This allows for more human involvement but insists that all "statements of science and history" in the Bible are true and exact.

Third, people accept the "balanced inerrancy" view. This perspective says "every word in scripture is the word God wanted," but God worked through human personalities, and we can see their humanity within the words. Dockery agrees the Bible writers sometimes rounded off numbers and dates and that sometimes the Bible meant for words to be taken in general rather than literal ways.

Fourth, some embrace what scholars call "limited inerrancy." This view says the Bible is inerrant in matters of salvation, ethics, faith, and practice. The inspiration of the Bible allows for misstatement in matters of science and history but not in areas of redemption.

Fifth, people believe in the "functional inerrancy" of the Bible. This view contends the Bible inerrantly accomplishes what God wanted it to do—reveal God and bring people into fellowship with him.[11]

Given the multiplicity of views, Baptists can respond in one of two ways. First, we can discover that everyone fits under one of these five categories. So, all of us can agree we're an inerrantist. I expect we'e all willing to do just that so long as the term isn't used to define a host of social and political issues as well. Or, we can say that the wide variance in the meaning of the word makes it essentially useless and we shouldn't insist on one word as the only way of describing the scriptures.

The Dynamic Theory and Balanced Inerrancy

I suspect Bill Stephens has correctly assessed the problem many of us face in his "Doctrine of the Bible" series written for the Baptist Sunday School Board in 1992. Stephens, using Dockery's book as a starting point, outlines Dockery's views of inerrancy and compares them to the dynamic theory of inspiration. Stephens wrote,

When dynamic inspiration is categorized as liberal, our hackles rise. And when plenary verbal is used to describe the view we grew up calling dynamic, we have trouble making the shift. . . . Balanced inerrancy is essentially what we have always believed and taught.[12]

Whichever term we use, we need to understand this point clearly—Baptists have lived and continued to live as Bible people. Notice what the plenary verbal and dynamic believers have in common. They all accept Jesus Christ as Lord and Savior. They all accept the need to follow the Bible in its direction for life. They all believe God communicates to us in the pages of scripture. They all seek to understand more fully the meaning of the text and how it applies to us.

On these points of commonality can we not allow individual Christians to decide what term they want to apply to their view of scripture? If we can, then we cannot also pull ourselves away from the tarbaby of distrust and personal animosity that threatens the fellowship of which we are a part?

In *East of Eden*, John Steinbeck described Lizzie Hamilton as a religious woman who read the Bible with great regularity. She treated the book with respect because it taught her history as well as poetry. From it she learned about people, ethics and morals, and salvation. Yet, she had one fatal flaw in her devotion to scripture: "She never studied the Bible or inspected it; she just read it. . . . And finally she came to the point where she knew it so well that she went right on reading it without listening."[13]

Baptists today have more need to listen to the Bible than to argue over it. We hold the Bible in high esteem but too quickly pay little attention to what it actually means. Too often we search it to uncover proof that backs up our own opinions. Or, we study it to find what we want to hear instead of what God wants to speak. The principle of Bible authority remains a foundation stone for us. Let's hear its call to "love one another" as a stepping stone beyond the arena of conflict into the world of ministry and edification.

Notes

[1]Hershel H. Hobbs, *The Baptist Faith and Message* (Nashville: Convention Press, 1971) 21.

[2]As cited in Joe T. Odle, *Why I Am a Baptist* (Nashville: Broadman Press, 1972) 94.

[3]Russell H. Dilday, Jr., *The Doctrine of Biblical Authority* (Nashville: Convention Press, 1982) 9.

[4]Hobbs, 22.

[5]Ibid.

[6]Ibid.

[7]Ibid., 28.

[8]W. A. Criswell, *Why I Preach That the Bible Is Literally True* (Nashville: Broadman Press, 1969) 26.

[9]Ibid., 49. Emphasis mine.

[10]Clark Pinnock, *The Scripture Principle* (San Francisco: Harper & Row, 1984) 58.

[11]David Dockery, *The Doctrine of the Bible* (Nashville: Convention Press, 1991) 86–87.

[12]Bill Stephens, as cited in *Florida Baptist Witness*, 6 February 1992, 12.

[13]John Steinbeck, *East of Eden* (New York: Bantam Books, 1955) 48f.

Chapter Four

Where Christ Is: The Autonomy of the Local Church

Matthew 18:20

A Well-Traveled Membership

On September 21, 1971, I walked the aisle of the First Baptist Church of Abbeville, South Carolina, and accepted Jesus Christ as my Savior and Lord. Two Sundays later I went forward again at the Coronaca Baptist Church in Greenwood, to join the church through believer's baptism.

In June of 1972, after my first semester as a student at Anderson College, I joined the First Baptist Church of Woodruff, South Carolina, to serve as their summer youth minister. Two years later, while a student at Furman University, I changed my membership to the First Baptist Church of Spartanburg, South Carolina, where I attended with a number of friends.

In April of 1977, my now-frayed membership card received another scratch on the edge when I became the associate pastor of the First Baptist Church of Denton, North Carolina.

After three years in Denton, I moved to Baylor University. Again my church membership moved with me. This time it landed at the Columbus Avenue Baptist Church in Waco, Texas. There it remained until June of 1982. At that time it flew East and ended up at the Warrenton Baptist Church in Warrenton, North Carolina. Following that, it moved to the Grace Baptist Church in Sumter, South Carolina. Now, finally, five years later, it has moved to the great midwest, to the First Baptist Church of Jefferson City, Missouri.

If my membership card could speak, it would tell us about the vast differences found in each one of these Southern Baptist churches. Each church looks different architecturally. The Abbeville church has a Gothic front, while the Coronaca, Spartanburg, Denton, Columbus Avenue, and Warrenton churches all have the typical Colonial style of columns and red brick. Grace bears its own distinctive architectural style with a domed top. The Woodruff church didn't even have a sanctuary in 1972. The congregation worshipped in an old fellowship hall, while a construction crew built the fellowship a sanctuary.

Not only were the churches different in architecture, they were also different in worship methods. Each church had a little different emphasis in music. The Coronaca church liked the "country gospel" sound, while the Warrenton choir never sang anything but high church classical music. In Warrenton the ministers who preceded me wore a robe into the pulpit. When I decided not to wear one, some members of the congregation thought the world had surely come to an end.

In Denton the deacons sat in chairs around the communion table during the Lord's Supper. At Columbus Avenue, the pastor invited a few friends, different each time, to sit with him at the communion table to help serve the elements.

I could continue for hours detailing for you the numerous variations in each Baptist congregation in which I have worshipped and served. From preaching styles, to Sunday School literature, to the functions of the deacons, to the amounts given to missions, all of these churches were different.

Autonomy Defined

Although I didn't know at first why they were so different, I recognized Baptist variations early in my Christian pilgrimage. Now, however, I know we have a high-sounding phrase and a long-standing doctrine to describe our local church distinctives. Baptist churches have proudly accepted such congregational diversity because we believe in what we call "the autonomy of the local church."

For the uninitiated reader, let me take a moment to explain what this term means. The word "autonomous" means "self-governing," "self-controlled," or "self-directed." When we say we believe in "local church autonomy," we're saying we believe the local congregation should determine its own method of faith and practice.

A number of practical implications arise from this doctrine. It means every church calls its pastor without influence from a governing body above it. It means each church worships in the form that best meets the needs of its particular group of members. It means each congregation chooses its level of participation in the efforts of the larger group of Baptists. It means the various local bodies determine what theology they believe necessary for its members to accept. In essence, the doctrine called "the autonomy of the local church" gives the local congregation freedom to live, worship, and serve as its membership chooses.

In *Baptist Polity: As I See It*, James Sullivan, former president of the Baptist Sunday School Board, said,

> Each church owns its own property, calls its own pastor, makes it own decisions and lives with them, observes the Lord's Supper, baptizes believers into its membership by standards that it considers the church mandates, ordains pastors and deacons, and many other things that are considered prerogatives of the local church.[1]

The Essentials for the Church

Fred Craddock, professor of preaching at the Candler School of Theology at Emory University, once told of visiting the governor's mansion in San Juan, Puerto Rico. In the entry hall, Craddock saw an antique chest sitting by the wall. He asked his host the history of the piece. The host told him the story. The chest, used by the ruling families in the past to hold the family valuables, was built in the 1700s. It had three keyholes in the front. The three keyholes prevented any *one* person from stealing the money and jewels placed in the chest. They also guaranteed that any thief outside the family had to locate three keys instead of one to complete a robbery.

Craddock used this image to say the church occurs when three spiritual events take place. Without any one of the three keys, the church doesn't exist and people cannot experience the treasures the Lord wants to share with them.

In Matthew 18:20, we find the three essentials for the establishment of a church. First, we discover the church is a community. "Where two or three are gathered (Matt 18:20a)," said Jesus, we find the church. The church doesn't exist in isolation. A holy man sitting on a rock contemplating God in a desert doesn't make a church. If we're not with other believers, we don't find the church.

Second, the church exists when the community gathers in "Christ's name." A group of people gathered around a noble ideal or a good work doesn't make the church. But, a group tied in the common belief that Jesus Christ is God's Son and our savior, does make the church.

Third, when people congregate in this belief, Christ comes to them. "There," spoke Jesus, "am I in the midst of them (Matt 18:20b)." The group experiences the dynamic presence of a living Lord. We need never ask God to be present with us because God faithfully encounters us in our act of coming together.

The church exists, then, wherever and whenever people join other people to worship the risen Lord. "Where Christ is," said Ignatius, the early church father and theologian, "there is the church!" The church doesn't need oversight from any ecclesiastical body to make it the church. It requires no convention approval to call pastors, ordain deacons, perform the ordinances, or activate its ministry. It is sufficient in and of itself.

Hershel Hobbs said it this way:

> The word "church" in the New Testament never refers to organized Christianity or to a group of churches. It denotes either a local body of baptized believers or includes all the redeemed through the ages. The greater emphasis among Baptists . . . is on the local church.[2]

Certainly, the congregations of the first century understood it this way. Anyone with even a cursory knowledge of the New

Testament knows how different each congregation was and how none tried to influence the form or method of the other.

In his letters to the churches, Paul never expected conformity, and he never advocated coercion. Each congregation experienced individual problems and celebrated individual victories. Paul never tried to create a set of guidelines that each church should use as it lived out its worship and ministry life. He didn't try to impose a uniform style of worship, doctrine, or structure upon local congregations. He recognized and respected the right of the local church to govern itself as it believed the Lord Jesus had commanded.

Autonomy Grounded in History

Baptists in general and Southern Baptists in particular have laid claim to the principle of church autonomy. Our founding constitution calls for a recognition and respect of this concept:

> While independent and sovereign in its own sphere, the convention does not claim and will never attempt to exercise any authority over any other Baptist body, whether church, auxiliary, organizations, association, or convention.[3]

Such has been our statement of belief. In recent years, however, a subtle, but steady, erosion of our stated principle has begun. Unless we watch for it, we will never see the erosion, but it is present.

When our convention leadership attacks any form of worship—liturgical or Pentecostal—or any type of music—classical or charismatic—used in Southern Baptist churches as illegitimate for spiritual people, the principle of autonomy suffers. In the last decade the more "formal" styles of music and worship have faced the greatest attack. Statements like, "You can't have high church music and warm hearted evangelism," and, "Liturgy always leads to lethargy," imply one worship style should replace another and pressure the congregation to one form in order to be an acceptable church.

We see the erosion of local church autonomy when unauthorized lay leadership in state conventions compiles computer list-

ings of so-called fundamentalist-conservative pastors and systematically sends resumes of such men to churches looking for
ministers. The effort to influence the local church toward a
particular stripe of theology and method damages the principle of
autonomy.

We see the erosion when associations begin to disfellowship
churches over such issues as calling a previously divorced pastor,
a charismatic pastor, or a woman pastor.

We see it when our national agencies cut off financial support
to any church that calls a pastor with either of these three decreed
liabilities against them.

Now, I'm not a woman. I don't speak in tongues. And I pray
to God I'll never experience the tragedy of a divorce. So, why am
I concerned about any of this? I'm concerned because I believe the
local church has the right to call whomever it chooses to serve as
its pastor unless that choice violates the clear mandate of scripture.

The issue boils down to this: do we genuinely believe that
when a group of "two or three are gathered together," there Christ
is "in the midst of them"? Even if I disagree vehemently with their
choices, my scripture and my Baptist heritage call me to respect
the right of congregations to govern themselves.

I like the way Paul Powell, formerly the pastor of the Green
Acres Baptist church in Tyler, Texas, and now the head of the
Southern Baptist Convention's Annuity Board, put it when he
spoke of the struggles within the Southern Baptist Convention. He
referred to associations disfellowshiping churches and said, "If we
keep thinning our ranks, soon there won't be anybody left but you
and me . . . and I'm not sure how long you are going to last."[4] If
we don't begin soon to respect the rights of the local church again,
we not only will trim our ranks but will destroy our principle of
autonomy.

Recently, a pastor friend told me of a deacons' meeting at his
church where they discussed a camp their deacons were planning
to attend for a training retreat. In the conversation, one of his
deacons correctly noted the camp wasn't sponsored by any state
or national Southern Baptist group. The deacon found some fault
with that and wanted to know what the pastor planned to do
about it.

The implication startled my friend. If it wasn't "sponsored" by an official Baptist body, then the inference was that maybe the deacons shouldn't do it.

I asked my friend, "What did you do?" He said, "I told my deacons I didn't care where a camp or a ministry program or a book or a film originated if it met the needs of my local congregation."

My friend's words remind us of something valuable in this era of tension between denominational authority and local church autonomy. The denomination exists to serve the churches, not the other way around. To imply anything else infringes upon the right of a congregation to choose its own direction in ministry and worship.

Autonomy means bottoms-up choices, not top-down directives. It means *churches* choose their literature, their programs and their missions emphases for themselves, rather than having denominations dictate these to them.

Autonomy and Cooperation

Obviously, most Baptist churches have practiced autonomy within the context of a cooperative spirit. Seeking to do together what the individual church couldn't do alone, our local churches have pooled resources to fund missions, to establish institutions like hospitals, colleges and seminaries, and to promote the Baptist view of faith.

The principle of autonomy can exist side by side with the practice of cooperation. This happens, however, only when two attitudes remain constant.

First, cooperation implies mutual respect. For example, suppose in a local association, 27 churches band together to begin a prison ministry. One of the churches in the association has ordained women deacons. The others haven't. In order to cooperate within autonomy, the churches have to respect the right of the other to govern itself. They may not agree with the choice, but to work together, they have to respect it.

Second, cooperation implies mutual involvement in the governance of ministries. Could we realistically expect the church that ordains women to continue to give leaders, workers, money, and support to the associational work with the prison if the association refuses to allow any members of that church to serve on the committees within the association? Cooperation within autonomy requires representation of all the self-governing churches involved.

The instant one church becomes intolerant of the beliefs and practices of a second one, the balance between autonomy and cooperation breaks down. Either the intolerant church will break fellowship over the alleged "error" of the sister congregation or the unacceptable church will cease to participate fully in the life of the association.

Autonomy lives constantly in tension with cooperation. A church can give up its autonomy in the interest of cooperation as easily as a cooperative church can insist upon its self-governance. In our present Southern Baptist Convention landscape, I suspect the former occurs much more often than the latter. We've become so enamored with the "success" of our cooperative venture, we've largely abdicated our autonomy out of a fear of disrupting it. Our modern Baptist family has largely abdicated its self-governance. We receive the word from on high—we purchase our literature, receive our programs and determine our theology from sources beyond our local congregation. Our cooperation has led to connectionalism, and our connectionalism has led, in some instances, to coercion.

Conformists and Autonomists

I think our commitment to the principle of local church autonomy has weakened because of the new vision so many people bring to our cooperative fellowship. This new vision directly conflicts with the one we've traditionally held. In our convention today our churches and their individual members embrace two different images of what we should be. I call these two groups the conformists and the autonomists.

The Conformists

The conformists see our Southern Baptist Convention as an *army on the march*. They dream of millions of troops marching lockstep in time. They want to hear the soldiers repeating identical orders of the day. They want the troops to wear uniforms of the same color, cloth, and insignia.

They desire allegiance to one commander. They want the soldiers to receive orders passed down through the ranks, from top to bottom. They see the Southern Baptist Convention as one column, as an indistinguishable mass, marching forward toward victory for God.

In this image individual churches and members lose their identity, their uniqueness, and their individuality because the leaders think this diversity leads to a lack of direction.

The Autonomists

The autonomists, however, see a different vision. They see our millions not as an army on the march, but as *a band of pilgrims on a journey*. Everyone is moving, but at different speeds. A drummer beats a rhythm, but not everyone hears it. A few even carry their own drums. This band scatters out across the field as its members walk. Three or four argue, then laugh at their disagreement. One stops to feed a hungry child. Another stoops to pick up an aged traveler. But, the march goes forward, even if it stops and starts.

In this band, no one forces anyone to march. Members wear clothes of many colors. They speak all at once sometimes. But, the march goes forward.

Listen. The drum beat isn't regular. The steps are out of time. But, with God urging them onward, the pilgrims continue to move. The only thing they have in common is that funny mark on their forehead. It looks like—it is—a cross! They all wear it. It binds them together. It identifies them. It makes them one in Christ. And the march goes on.[5]

God's Invitation

God invites all of us to join his army. He invites all of his autonomous churches to cooperate in his struggle against sin and evil and pain and injustice.

But, today the conformists have become the generals of the army. They order conformity, with the risk of censure for those who refuse to march to their tune. They ask not for cooperation, which has long been our model, but subjugation, which, hopefully will never become our model.

Yet, I hear God calling again—calling for us to listen to his voice of command and none other than his. He calls us to freedom as churches, not to conformity. He wants us to work together but not to melt together as churches or as individuals.

So, let's get on with the march. But, let's wear our own clothes and listen to our own music and plot our own course. That course may call us away, to a different path than that down which the army in lockstep is heading. But, that's okay. I would rather follow Christ than some duly elected general any day! Wouldn't you? As long as "two or three are gathered together, there Christ is in the midst of them."

Notes

[1]James Sullivan, *Baptist Polity: As I See* It (Nashville:Broadman Press, 1983) 258.

[2]Hershel Hobbs, *The Baptist Faith and Message* (Nashville: Broadman Press, 1971) 75.

[3]Cited in Burtt Potter, Jr., *Baptists: The Passionate People* (Nashville: Broadman Press, 1973) 63.

[4]Cited from a sermon preached at the Baptist General Convention of Texas in November, 1987.

[5]The image of the "pilgrims on the march," which I've used here, originated with Elizabeth O'Connor, *Search For Silence* (San Diego: Luramedia, 1986) 56–57.

Chapter Five

Faith Without a Wall:
No Lord But Christ,
No Creed But the Bible

Acts 2:36–39

The Destruction of a Castle

In the convention sermon of 1988, Dr. Joel Gregory, the former pastor of the First Baptist Church in Dallas, Texas, related the story of the unusual destruction of an ancient Irish castle. The castle owners had moved away from it years before and thick weeds and green vines now covered the once smooth face of the stone.

Not surprisingly, the local peasants took advantage of the absentee owners and began to use the finely shaped stones of the castle for their own purposes. When they needed stone for a road, a chimney, a wall, or a home, they chipped it from the castle and hauled it away.

One day, Lord Londonderry, the last surviving member of the family that had built the castle, returned to the home of his ancestors. Seeing the marks of the peasant's destruction, he immediately contacted a construction agent and instructed him to build a wall around the castle high enough to keep the peasants and trespassers out. Confident the job would be done, Londonderry returned to the city.

Three years later he went back to see his castle again. To his amazement, the castle had vanished. Surrounding the spot where the castle had stood was a sturdy wall—thick and threatening. But, the wall enclosed nothing.

Londonderry sent for his construction agent and asked him "Where is the castle?" The engineer replied, "The castle? I thought you wanted a wall! I built the wall with the stones from the castle. Why should I travel many miles and pay good money for rock when the finest stones in Ireland were right here beside me?"

Lord Londonderry had his wall, but the castle, without which the wall meant nothing, had been destroyed in the process.[1]

Gregory used this illustration to state two emphases. First, he warned Southern Baptists not to destroy their Southern Baptist castle in their efforts to build an orthodox theological wall. Second, he suggested that the Southern Baptist Convention could build its wall and keep its castle. In his message, Gregory offered a method to guide us.

I appreciated Dr. Gregory's message, but one concern in it stood out to me. Until a few years ago, we never saw the need to surround ourselves with a wall! We believed the Bible was creed enough.

A History of No Walls

Anyone with any knowledge of Baptist history and polity recognizes our complete aversion to wall-building. Baptists have long declared, "No Lord but Christ, no creed but the Bible.
Let me share a few quotes that demonstrate the historical Baptist position.

Billy Graham said of Baptists, "Their creed, their discipline, their rules of faith and practice have historically been the Bible."[2]

Grady Cothen said, "To the degree we try to write and enforce creedal statements, we compromise our Baptist distinctive."[3]

In his book describing the *Baptist Faith and Message* statement of 1963, Dr. Hershel Hobbs wrote of the Baptist aversion to "official" statements of faith. "Baptists have always shied away from anything that resembled a creed or a statement of beliefs to which their people were forced to subscribe."[4]

Hobbs continued, "One may safely say that there is no such thing as an official statement of faith and message among Southern Baptists.[5] Finally, Hobbs stated the *Baptist Faith and Message* is information and guidelines, not a creed. Some of the Convention's agencies and institutions have agreed to use this statement as an expression of their faith. But they have done so voluntarily, not by a vote of the Convention itself. Indeed, the New Orleans (1969) and the Denver (1970) Conventions refused to make acceptance of this statement mandatory upon its institutions and agencies or upon those who work for and/or with them. Thus it remained firm at this point in its belief in the competency of the soul in religion.[6]

A Shift In Perspective

Unfortunately, the evidence now demonstrates a willingness to develop creedal tests of faith for involvement and leadership in the Southern Baptist Convention. In the last decade the neo-Baptists in the Southern Baptist Convention, those who now control our agencies and institutions, have systematically begun the task of building a creedal wall around our Southern Baptist castle. Fearful of perceived, but never identified, liberal peasants, these psuedo-Baptists have initiated and pretty much completed efforts at the Home Mission Board, at our six Baptist seminaries, at the Christian Life Commission, and now at the Foreign Mission Board, to tighten the theological screws on administrators, teachers, and missionaries who serve with these agencies. Especially have the neo-Baptists initiated policies to determine the strict orthodoxy of any new leaders and employees of these agencies and institutions.

Using the *Baptist Faith and Message* statement of 1963 and the so-called "Peace Committee Report of 1987" (and their own self-conceived interpretations of them) as their measuring sticks of orthodoxy, Southern Baptist creedalists seek to abolish the long-cherished Baptist doctrine, "No Lord But Christ, No Creed But The Bible." Not trusting Baptists in the pews to read the scriptures for themselves and reach their own doctrines under the dynamic power of the Holy Spirit, these static Baptists want to reduce religious experience to an agreement with a system of codified and decreed statements of faith. They show in their actions and words a preference for law over grace, bondage over freedom, a wall over a castle.

A number of recent events and statements demonstrate the unprecedented drive toward creedalism. In the spring of 1992,

Keith Parks, then President of the Foreign Mission Board, decided to retire. He gave several reasons for his retirement. Parks said, "One reason was the denomination was moving from a confessional to a creedal body.[7]

Also in 1992, a number of new professors and a dean were elected by the trustees at The Southern Baptist Theological Seminary. Under questioning, the trustees were surprised to learn the new professors accepted the notion of women serving as deacons and even pastors. One of the trustees said later, "If we can get men who are 95 percent correct, why can't we get men who are 100 percent correct?"[8]

At Southeastern Baptist Theological Seminary, the trustees have voted to amend the charter and to incorporate the language of "biblical inerrancy" as the statement of faith necessary for all new professors to accept. I could give other examples of the creedal shift in the Southern Baptist Convention. These should suffice, though, to show we're living in a new era—the era when human mediators intervene and add words and interpretations to the scriptures and make them the basis for involvement and leadership within the Southern Baptist Convention.

A Biblical Basis For Faith and Fellowship

In Acts 2:36-41, the scriptures give us the first sermon of the church. Peter preached it to a crowd gathered in Jerusalem. His words convicted the listeners. They asked, "What shall we do?" Peter told them, "Repent and be baptized in the name of Jesus Christ." They obeyed and 3, 000 were baptized as a result of their faith.

This text describes for us the only doctrinal profession necessary for any person to enter into a full salvation experience with Jesus Christ and into a full fellowship with a Baptist congregation. From it, I offer you four simple, but profound, requirements for salvation and fellowship.

First, we *accept our personal need for a Savior.* In verse 38 Peter encouraged his hearers to "repent . . . for the remission, of sins." If we don't recognize "all have sinned and fallen short of the glory of God (Rom 3:23)," if we don't understand our own moral and spiritual failures, then we cannot and will not turn away from them in genuine Christian repentance.

Second, *we acknowledge Jesus Christ as the resurrected Lord*. Acts 2:36 tells us, "Let all the house of Israel know that God has made Jesus, whom you crucified, both Lord and Christ." The entire context of the preceding verses reminds us, God "raised up" Christ (vv. 24, 32). Without his victory over death we possess no power over the penalty of sin.

Third, we *believe in Jesus Christ as the only Savior capable of freeing us from our bondage to our* sins. We believe in the cross as the high-priced gift that God offered for us to bear our penalty himself. When Peter exhorted the Jerusalem listeners to "be baptized in the name of Jesus Christ for the remission of sins," he left no doubt about the unique power of the crucified Christ to free our hands and hearts from the life-killing chains of evil. Only Jesus can break those chains and to him we must go if we're to know salvation.

Fourth, *we openly and publicly embrace the Christ who so graciously forgives us*. In this phrase "be baptized," Peter understood, as did his congregation, the public nature of Christian faith. He didn't imply that baptism assured salvation. But, he did believe that salvation implied voluntary profession, through baptism, of Jesus Christ. When a person experienced baptism in the early church, the person willingly stood before the body of believers and acknowledged "Jesus Christ is Lord, to the glory of God the Father." That was all the profession required then, and that remains our only necessary profession today.

Often we share in the baptism of new believers into our local congregations. Everyone of those baptized should understand the four points I just mentioned. But, most of them know little or nothing about hypostatic union, plenary verbal inspiration, the modalistic view of the Trinity, the substitutionary atonement, or the *plerosis* and *kenosis* of Christ. Yet, following their baptism, we accept them fully as Christians and as Baptists.

When I walked the aisle 20 years ago to accept Christ, and when you stepped down it to begin your Christian experience, neither the pastor nor the church required you to pass any doctrinal, creedal test before you became a part of the fellowship. No one asked you a lot of theological questions. What they asked you was something like this, "Do you accept Jesus as your Savior?" You said, "Yes," and they accepted you, based on that statement of faith. No more and no less! Following the scriptural pattern we have consistently rejected efforts to build a creedal wall around our fellowship.

I'm not saying we don't need doctrines as guidelines for our faith and our denomination. But, I am saying we've never before made creedal doctrines a test for, or a requirement for, entrance into our Baptist castle. We've never before made creedal doctrine a basis for employment in our agencies and institutions. Yes, we've had statements of faith and articles of confession. But until the last twelve years we've used them loosely, giving people freedom of interpretation. Now, we're using them as weapons to threaten our present leaders and as barriers to prevent others from entry into the Baptist system of leadership and employment.

Reasons to Reject a Wall

Using Gregory's parable of the castle and remembering the words of Peter, I want to outline five reasons why we should continue to reject the temptation to build a wall of creedalism around our Baptist castle.

Let God Defend the Castle

First, we *should not build a wall because we don't need it if the owner of the castle lives in the* castle. When I heard Dr. Gregory's sermon, I was haunted by the thought: "The owner should live in his castle if he wants it to survive."

If God lives within the Southern Baptist Convention, in its people, in its churches, in its agencies and institutions, God will defend the castle himself! Jesus Christ doesn't need our weak creedal walls to protect his spirit, his message, his scriptures, his gospel. The statement, "No Lord but Christ" reminds us that Jesus is quite capable of protecting his own interests. For us to think we need to build a wall around God's castle assumes God has either moved out or has grown weak in his own defense. I'm not ready to believe either of these possibilities. We don't need a wall because the landlord who originally built the castle and who has protected it to this point still resides in it in all of his glory and power.

Only Humans Build Walls

Second, *we should reject a creedal wall because the construction of one requires a builder other than God.* When a humanly constructed creed or confession takes the place of, or tries to define and interpret, a God-given document, the human statement always reflects a subjective, fallible, narrow viewpoint. That's why Baptists demand, "No Creed but the Bible." Any statement we make about the Bible, any word we use to describe the Bible that it doesn't use to describe itself, any doctrine we enforce concerning the Bible, automatically becomes tinged with the dirty fingerprints of our imperfections, our biases, and our inconsistencies.

As one writer put it,

> Since the creed is simply a statement of doctrinal belief and since it is written by human beings, it needs revision, updating, and correction. In the final analysis, the creed is little more than a human interpretation of God's word. Humans are always fallible.[10]

When we begin to write our creeds, we have to ask, "Who will compose them?" The answer is inevitable. "People will." Imperfect, finite, and prone-to-bias people become the builders of the wall. Thus, the wall always has flaws, even if the builders refuse to admit them.

In reality, a human effort to build a wall demonstrates an unbelievable arrogance. To think we can create something more sufficient than the Bible effectively puts the Bible in a secondary position of authority!

In the introduction to the *Baptist Faith and Message* statement, the writers recognized this reality. So, they wrote

> We do not regard them [statements of faith and doctrine] as ... having any quality of finality or infallibility ... the sole authority for faith and practice among Baptists is the scriptures of the Old and New Testaments. Confessions are only guides in interpretation, having no authority over the conscience. .... Such statements have never been regarded as ... official creeds carrying mandatory authority.[11]

We should reject the building of a wall because human statements deny the power of God to speak to us through the Bible alone. The Bible read, studied, and lived is creed enough. It always has been, and it always should be.

Walls Need Protectors

We should reject a doctrinal wall, thirdly, because *the construction of one means we also will need a protector of it.* After all, once the builder built the wall around the castle, what prevented the peasants from chipping stones away from it? The owner could protect the wall in one of two ways. He could build another wall around the first one. In other words, we have to tighten the creed again and again and again. Or, he could protect the wall by hiring a police force to stand guard over it.

Unfortunately, we now hear of a number of self-appointed "policemen" guarding our new creedal wall in the Southern Baptist Convention. Trustees at our seminaries now debate whether or not students should have the right to bring tape recorders into the classrooms even when the professors object. The policemen have arrived to record any professorial theological slippage.

The trustees at our missionary agencies are changing policies (or have already changed them) to involve themselves more directly in the interview process for our missionary candidates. Not trusting the personnel hired to do such investigations, the trustees, for the first time in history, interject their standards of orthodoxy into the calling process. This way they can identify non-creedalists and purge those who don't toe the neo-Baptist line. The police have arrived to screen out the moderates.

Only two years ago, Jerry Johnson, a young proponent of the new orthodoxy, declared of Dr. Roy Honeycutt, then the president of The Southern Baptist Theological Seminary, "A person would have to be blind as a mole not to see that Honeycutt doesn't believe the Bible.'" The policemen have arrived to check the conformity to the creed of all of us.

But I wonder: "Who appointed these new policemen to act as the judges of another person's conscience before God? Who made these enforcers the theological gate keepers to our faith? Who bestowed omniscience upon their powers of reason?"

Our creedal wall has already spawned a legion of protectors and enforcers. The suspicion and mistrust sown in such an atmosphere have virtually destroyed all semblance of Christian and Baptist unity.

Hobbs' words in *The Baptist Faith and Message* are highly prophetic. He wrote in 1971,

> In all likelihood the only thing that would divide Southern Baptists with regard to their faith would be for one group—to the right or left of center or even in the center—to attempt to force upon others a creedal faith.[13]

This effort to devise and implement a creed upon our institutions and agencies has brought us to this sad point of pain and fragmentation.

A Wall Closes off the Home

We reject a creedal wall, fourth, because *a wall always destroys the freedom to enter the home inside.* Growing up in Greenwood, South Carolina, I often passed a colonial brick house on my way to the baseball park nearby. A wall at least eight feet high surrounded the two story home. Black, iron spikes topped off the wall. I didn't know anything about the owners of the home except one thing. I knew they didn't want anyone to come inside their gates.

I also remember another home. It was also a red brick with Georgian columns. It, however, had nothing around it. In fact, it had a concrete pad in the back with a basketball goal set up right at the street corner. I'm sure you can guess which house attracted the most young people. We walked quickly by the foreboding wall, but we stopped often to play in the yard of the accessible home.

Given time, the neo-Baptists in our midst can build a wall of doctrine high enough and thick enough that no one will want to come inside and play in our yard. Instead of inviting lost peasants into our Baptist home, we're constructing walls of orthodoxy and conformity and creedalism which blocks them out.

A Wall Keeps People From Seeing the Landlord

Finally, we should reject the creedal wall *because it will inevitably block the view of the people who want to see the owner who lives within* it. I'm always amused at the efforts of the rich and famous to stay private. They build high fences, install alarm systems, and hire security guards. They don't want outsiders to see them. Yet, somehow, the photographers press ahead to snap their ill-gotten pictures of the "high and mighty." Photographers climb trees, rent helicopters, and charter boats to help them get in position to peer over the walls to see the famous people inside.

When we build our creedal walls we keep people away from seeing Jesus Christ. The wall takes the attention from Jesus. People don't want to see a wall! They don't even want to see the castle. People primarily want to catch a glimpse of the landlord, and a wall prevents them from viewing him.

I don't know who said it first but our Southern Baptist Convention would do well to heed these words again today: "The main thing is to keep the main thing the main thing!"

And what is the main thing? Is the main thing we want to share with a lost world our various theories of inspiration about the Bible? No. Is the main thing we want to share with a drugged world our divergent views about the authority of the pastor? No. Is the main thing we want to share with a frightened world our conflicting perspectives on women's ordination? No.

What is the main thing we want to share with a sin-sick world? We want to tell them God loves them. We want to tell them they're lost in their sins without Jesus. We want to tell them the cross and resurrection offer them a way to meaningful and eternal life. This message was and always should be our main thing. Jesus told us, "If I be lifted up I will draw all men to myself (John 12:32)."

It pains me say it, but many of our Baptist brethren are so busy building the wall that they've neglected the owner of the castle. In the last decade or so, the neo-Baptists have spent more time talking about the wall than they have about Jesus Christ. They've forced all of us to lose sight of the main thing.

The Openness of the Gospel

History tells us the Christian city of Constantinople fell to the Turks in 1495. Legend reports that while the Moslem hordes scaled the walls of the city on the outside, Christian monks debated theology on the inside. While the city fell, the monks argued over the sex of the angels, the color of the virgin Mary's eyes, and whether a fly that fell into holy water would be sanctified or the water polluted.

Our world races toward the darkness of an eternal night at warp speed. Addict mothers give birth to children already hooked to a destructive drug. Our inner cities burn with racism and sexism and unemployment. Our environment loses its ozone layer and dozens of species of plant and animal life each year. People who don't know the love of Christ live and die within steps of our churches without a witness of the gospel.

Yet, our Southern Baptist wall builders are guilty of the same kind of mindless speculation as the Christians in Constantinople. Men and women and boys and girls are crying out in their need for God and for each other. But many can't hear them because the neo-Baptists among us are busy playing theological trivial pursuit! And, they're trying to force us to play it with them.

Thankfully, however, a significant number of Baptists have said, "Enough!" They've said, "We will not live in your man-made fortresses of creed." This group wants to get away from wall-building. They want to remind Baptists in the pews that it is not the wall that's important. In fact, it's not even the castle that's important. Instead, it's the landlord, Jesus Christ, who deserves our ultimate allegiance.

The doctrine "No Lord But Christ, No Creed But The Bible" stands without a wall. Its gift is freedom. It invites people to meet the landlord and, because they know him, to enter the castle. The creedalists, however, go on building, protecting, and hiding behind their man-made walls. They don't believe knowing the landlord is sufficient. They tell you to scale the wall as well.

My Bible tells me they are wrong. My Bible tells me knowing Christ as Lord makes me a Christian and gives me entry into the Baptist castle.

Notes

[1] The sermon was reprinted in the *Baptist Standard* of Texas, 29 June 1988.

[2] Joe T. Odle, comp., *Why I Am A Baptist* (Nashville: Broadman Press, 1972) 17.

[3] Ibid., 73.

[4] Hobbs, *Baptist Faith and Message*, 13.

[5] Ibid., 15.

[6] Ibid., 15–16.

[7] Cited in *The Baptist Recorder*, 4 April 1992, 8.

[8] Cited in *The Word and Way*, 7 May 1992, 4.

[9] Cited in *The Florida Baptist Witness*, 24 October 1991, I discussed the term "inerrancy" in the chapter on biblical authority.

[10] Odle, *Why I Am A Baptist*, 54.

[11] Hobbs, Ibid., 2.

[12] Cited in *The Baptist Standard*, 2 May 1990, 8.

[13] Hobbs, Ibid., 11.

Chapter Six

Staying Out
of the Wrong Bed:
Separation
of Church and State

1 Kings 22: 1–9; 13–18; 24–28

The Unholy Alliance

The battle for the crown of Rome would begin at daybreak. Constantine, one of three men fighting for the crown, tossed uneasily upon his bed. A dream had awakened him from a troubled sleep. In his dream a flaming cross burned in the sky. Beneath the cross, Constantine read the words written in blood, "With this Conquer." Accepting this sign as a mandate from God, the previously pagan military ruler embraced Christianity as his new faith and eventually triumphed over his enemies and became Emperor of Rome.

In thanksgiving to God, he decreed religious freedom for Christians in A. D. 313. Then, from that moment, Constantine used the powers of the Roman State to force Christian faith upon his subjects. Christianity, which had been outlawed, now became the official religion of the Roman Empire. Once dread enemies, church and state now became bedfellows. People who refused to accept Christianity were persecuted by the state and the church. The church adopted the political philosophy of the state and the nation supported through its laws the religious outlook of the church. So it remained until the Reformation of the sixteenth century.

The Winds of Separation

Out of the Reformation, however, the winds of freedom blew. Out of the belief that every person was responsible for his or her own faith before God came the necessary corollary that no one, not even the king, had the right to dictate religious beliefs to the individual or to the church.

In England especially, the notion of a free church in a free state took root. In 1612, one of the first Baptists, Thomas Helwys, went to prison to die because he dared question the right of King James I to force people into the Anglican church by state decree. In 1660, King Charles I arrested John Bunyan, the Baptist of Bedford, and sent him to prison for 12 years because he insisted on the principle of separation of state and church.

Meanwhile, in the colonies of America, an upstart named Roger Williams became increasingly concerned as he watched the state-supported churches of Massachusetts punish people for refusing to accept the dogma of the Puritan faith. His public sermons against such coercive practices led to a trial against him. The charge "entertaining dangerous opinions" won out, and the civil and religious authorities banished Williams for his convictions.

Moving to the largely unsettled area of Rhode Island, Williams embraced the Baptist faith and championed the notion that a person could worship or not worship as they chose without coercion from the state or the church. Under Williams' leadership the compact of Rhode Island gave the individual person freedom from the dictates of the state in religious matters. For the first time since Constantine the unholy marriage between church and state was dissolved.

Gradually, the idea that church and state should be separate defeated the Catholic model of church and state wed together and came to dominate not only the government and churches of the United States, but also those of several other democratic nations. Baptists were the major instigators in this movement toward freedom, insisting that the church leave the secular sphere to the government and that the state leave the religious arena to the church.

The Baptist Position

We should point proudly, therefore, to the fact that Baptists gave birth to this principle. The doctrine of the separation of church and state is one of our children. In the book, *Why I Am A Baptist*, Joe Odle quotes the historian Frank S. Mead concerning Baptists and the separation of church and state:

> Complete separation of church and state! They have never been a state church, have never taken orders from the government or king; . . . freedom of conscience and complete divorce of church and state. How they have suffered for that! They have faced mockery and mud, fines, whippings, and iron bars; they have been burned at the stakes and pulled at the rack, but they have held to it.[1]

Traditionally then, Baptists have believed that the church should not expect the state to force belief and that the government should not expect the church blindly to support its policies and programs.

Herschel Hobbs, a longtime patriarch of Baptist belief, shares four implications of this doctrine for us in *The Baptist Faith and Message*. First, "The church should not seek to use the state for its purposes." Second, "the state should not commandeer the church for political ends." Third, "The state should not favor one church above another." Fourth, "Church and state are mutually exclusive."[2]

The Wall Erodes

Unfortunately, in the last several years, the historic Baptist insistence upon this doctrine has come under increasing attack. Let me list only a few examples of the attack. In 1984, in a televised interview with Bill Moyers, W. A. Criswell called the notion of the separation of church and state "the figment of some infidel's imagination."[3] In 1984, the Southern Baptist Convention, meeting in Kansas City, refused to approve a strong resolution against the appointment of an ambassador to the Roman Catholic Church because, as our leadership put it, it might "embarrass the president." In 1948 when Harry Truman tried the same thing, we filed a lawsuit with a number of other religious bodies to stop the President's effort.

In 1987, the Baptist Public Affairs Committee publicly endorsed a candidate for political appointment for the first time in Baptist history. A number of Baptist leaders called the action "unprecedented" and "dangerous." In 1991 and 1992, the Christian Life Commission called for a new discussion of the possibility of "vouchers or tuition tax credits" from the government being given to parents of students attending private, religious schools. The Christian Life Commission did this in spite of Baptists' previously adopted positions in conventions against this (in 1974, 1975, 1978, and 1982).[4]

Finally, in 1991, the new leadership in our convention completed their efforts to defund completely the Baptist Joint Committee on Public Affairs. They did so primarily because the leader of the Baptist Joint Committee, James Dunn, refused to give up the principle called separation of church and state.

Historically, Baptists didn't care much where a brother or sister stood in their politics. They did care, however, when a group from any political and theological perspective, right or left, tried to dominate our convention to accomplish political goals. They did care when such actions threatened our cherished doctrine of separation of church and state.

Certainly, every Christian wants to respond appropriately to the need to be involved in the political arena. We should participate in the process so we can insure our values and beliefs will receive a hearing in our national life. But, involvement doesn't mean manipulation of our churches and our convention for the benefit of any secular political party.

A Biblical Model

With this history and these implications hanging in the air as a backdrop, I want to turn our attention to a passage of scripture from 1 Kings 22. In this text we find an example of what can occur when religious leaders and political leaders cozy up too closely to one another.

Let me refresh your memory of the details of the situation. A land-hungry king named Ahab had cast his eyes and set his cap for a piece of territory called Ramoth-Gilead. Unfortunately for Ahab, another bunch of tough guys, led by their king Aram, had a pretty firm grip on that particular neck of the woods.

Ahab, however, called in a friend, a fellow Hebrew, Jehoshaphat by name, and asked him to "partner up" with him to wrest the land from the people of Aram. In their conversation Jehoshaphat wanted to know "What advice are your religious leaders giving you about this?"

Responding to Jehoshaphat's question, Ahab sent a messenger to bring back his court prophets. In they trooped, 400 strong, to offer their counsel. Ahab asked these so-called religious leaders, "Shall I go or refrain?" With one voice they told him what he wanted to hear. I can hear their unison voices now, "Go, for the Lord will give it unto the hand of the king."

You would think the advice of these 400 religious types would have satisfied Jehoshaphat. But apparently, he smelled something fishy. He figured out the obvious. These religious men were tied closely to the king. So, he asked a second time, "Is there not yet a prophet of the Lord, that we may inquire of him?"

Ahab dreaded this question. "Yes," he sadly replied. "There's a guy named Micaiah, but I hate him. He's always criticizing me. He never speaks well of me." Reluctantly then, Ahab called for Micaiah. In answer to the same question, "Shall I go or refrain?" Micaiah sarcastically replied, "Go up and the Lord will deliver it into your hands."

Ahab caught the sarcasm and ordered Micaiah to say what he truly felt. This time Micaiah pronounced, "I saw Israel scattered on the mountains like sheep who have no master." In other words, Ahab will die and Israel will lose.

As Micaiah concluded his vision of the destruction of Israel's army, Zedekiah, leader of the court prophets, smacked Micaiah across the face and Ahab ordered the Lord's lonely prophet into prison.

Reasons to Reject the Suitor

This text illustrates for us the dangers of a marriage between government and religion.

Loss of Independence

First, *the church loses its independent voice as God's judge upon government when it has tied itself to the rulers of that government.* The 400 prophets in Ahab's court couldn't risk "embarrassing" their king so they refused to speak the truth. They lost their freedom to speak out against the evil of Ahab when they became mouthpieces for the government rather than spokespersons for God.

We want no misunderstanding on this point. Christians love our government. 1 Timothy 2:15 exhorts us to pray for our leaders. We're probably more patriotic than any other segment of our population. But we dare not allow our love for our nation to silence our voice for God. Jesus told us "to render unto Caesar that which is Caesar's, and unto God that which is God's!" Our government deserves our citizenship but not our worship. When we see evil in our system, whether it's corruption in the Pentagon, lack of ethics in the House of Representatives, misuse of the Judicial branch, or influence-peddling in the White House, we must retain the freedom to voice our godly discontent.

If we allow any group or any party to commandeer our denomination for their political ends, as Ahab did these court prophets, we will fall mute out of reverence for government and neglect of God.

Baptists need to recognize the realities. The temptation of the church is to want the government to legitimize its belief and its moralities. We're tempted to try to use the government (or to control it through a particular political party) in the effort to gain legitimacy.

On the other hand, the government (a party in leadership or seeking leadership) will seek to use the church (or a segment of the church) in the effort to gain a constituency. The church wants legitimacy. The party wants a constituency. That's where the danger arises.

The Coattail Might Rip

A marriage between government and religion also hurts our religious witness because the *failure of the political group leads also to the failure of the religious body.* I wonder what happened to the 400 court prophets who told Ahab, "Go up to Ramoth-Gilead for the Lord will deliver it into your hands." Certainly, they were discredited in the eyes of the people. Surely, they were removed from their positions. Usually, in cases like those, they were executed. When their king failed, they lost their status, they lost their popularity, and they lost their opportunity to influence people for God.

It doesn't matter what your individual politics might be. But, it makes all of Christianity look foolish when we wrap our arms around any political candidate as "God's instrument" or as "God's Christian candidate." We've embraced candidates in the past, with preachers from the liberal side and preachers from the fundamentalist side endorsing specific individuals from their pulpits. Then, those preachers have watched in agony as time and events revealed sexual indiscretions, private profanity, the practice of astrology, and a total lack of church involvement as characteristics of these men once named "God's choice."

The cause of Christ always loses when we publicly endorse personalities or parties from the pulpits of our churches or from the platforms of our denominational meetings.

A Child Called "Intolerance"

The marriage between politics and religion spawns a third danger. *The offspring of the two is always religious and political intolerance for the person in the minority.* In our text Zedekiah, the high priest of the political ruler, demonstrated his intolerance when he struck Micaiah. The government showed its intolerance as Ahab threw Micaiah into prison for his honesty in speaking for God.

The key ingredient to the mixture of a free church in a free state is the spice labeled tolerance. When we tie the state and the church together, however, the church uses civil power to enforce its brand of religion, and the government appropriates the name of God for its brand of politics. Anyone who disagrees with either faces censure and persecution.

Whether we like it or not we live in a pluralistic nation. over 2,000 religious groups practice their beliefs in the United States. In a number of northern and industrial states, the Catholic church dominates. In one state the majority of its citizens cite Buddhism as the religious preference. Another marks "no religion" as the choice of most. In at least one state Mormonism predominates. In most Southern states, Southern Baptists thrive as the majority. So, in our denomination and in our nation today we need to answer these questions: "Will we tolerate other religious views? Will we give a person the right to believe nothing if they so choose?"

When Baptists suffered as a minority, we championed such freedom because we were the ones who felt the heavy hand and harsh whip of the religious oppressors. Now, however, Southern Baptists in the South reign as the cultural majority, even if not as the numerical one. I wonder, "Will we continue to grant others the right to believe and to speak, even when it crosses the grain of our particular view?"

The issue of tolerance or intolerance for the minority person comes to focus explicitly in the complex matter of government imposed school prayer. I think we can all agree we want our children to pray in school. I know I want mine to pray. But, I want them to pray what and when they choose, not when a school administrator or teacher forces them to pray.

I agree with the wag who said, "We'll always have prayer in schools. As long as we have tests, believe me, we'll have prayer."

But, let's have prayers that flow freely to God from our students, not prayers that the government forces the student to offer unto him.

If we force anyone to pray, we face three questions: "Who will write the prayer? Who will pray the prayer? What will we do with the one who doesn't want to pray?" I find it ironic that people who generally claim to want the government "off the backs of the people" so willingly invite the government to intrude into their religious lives by mandating school prayer.

The Godly Minority

Micaiah's experience teaches us a vital lesson. He was only one man against a government and a religious body unified in opposition to him. That's a definite minority. He suffered for his faith. But, God was on his side. As I think about it, Micaiah and Roger Williams and John Bunyan and Thomas Helwys had a lot in common.

As I think about it further, all of these had a lot in common with a man called Jesus. If you recall, the Roman government flexed the brunt of their muscle against him. If you recall, the Jewish religious system directed its intolerant power against him as well. Together, the Jewish Pharisees and the Roman government officials crucified Jesus because they couldn't tolerate his voice speaking out for God.

Nothing good ever happens when government and church try to use each other to accomplish their individual goals. The marriage always sires intolerance as its heir.

Bill Moyers, when a commentator for CBS news, once said, "Politics and religion separate but equal is the genius of the American system. But politics and religion together are poison which is to be avoided at all costs." We would do well to heed his warning.

Notes

[1]Joe T. Odle, *Why I Am a Baptist* (Nashville: Broadman Press, 1972) 109.

[2]Hershel H. Hobbs, *The Baptist Faith and Message* (Nashville: Broadman Press, 1971) 142.

[3]Cited in the *Baptist New Mexican*, 20 October 1984.

[4]As recorded in *The Word and Way*, 6 June 1992, 2.

Chapter Seven

A Man and a Tank:
The Right of Dissent

1 Kings 18

An Act of Dissent

No one knows the man's name. But few will ever forget his courage. He stood motionless in the street near Tiananmen Square in Peking, China, in June of 1989. Days of rioting and student protests and hunger strikes had thrown China into an unprecedented turmoil. Fearful of the hundreds of thousands of students who flooded the streets with banners and high hopes for democracy, China's hard-line leaders had ordered a crackdown. Deng Xiaoping, the aged leader of the totalitarian regime, sent the troops into the square and signaled the tanks to roll.

Roll they did. But not over this man. He held something in his hand, but it wasn't a gun. No, even a gun couldn't help him here. The man stared nose to muzzle with a line of armored tanks. A cameraman snapped the confrontation and froze it on film for all the world to see. The image of that slender Chinese student facing down a steel monster symbolized the struggle of a whole people seeking freedom in a Communist land. Defying all odds, he dissented against an authoritarian government.

Born in the Prisons

Not too many modern Baptists ever faced a tank determined to shut off their dissent. Our early Baptists ancestors, however, faced constant physical danger because they stood up for their beliefs against the power of an established government and church. Our history shows us that we were birthed near the beginning of the sixteenth century. At that time, the British government demanded allegiance to the Anglican Church. Baptists refused to give it. They refused for two main reasons. First, they rejected infant baptism as scriptural. They believed only those who had consciously accepted Jesus Christ as Lord should undergo the waters of belief. Second, they believed the government shouldn't dictate how a person should worship.

These staunch Baptists wanted liberty from coercive governmental interference in religious affairs. We were birthed in the labor pains of dissent and civil disobedience. Early Baptists lived as radicals against the government and the church of England. They were known as both traitors to the state and heretics of the church. They were the "agitators," the "dissenters" who stirred the waters in an effort to wash away the status quo.

Even a cursory reading of our history reveals to us our strife-torn origin. From John Smyth and Thomas Helwys, the English Baptists who fled London to Holland in 1607 to escape persecution at the hands of King James I; to John James, a General Baptist who was executed, then had his head displayed on a pole beside his church in 1661; to Roger Williams, who fled to America and eventually established the colony of Rhode Island as a place free from all religious coercion in 1644; Baptists faced the iron rule of law.[1]

In *Not a Silent People*, Walter Shurden, chairman of the department of Christianity at Mercer University wrote: "Baptists did more than merely talk. They acted. Baptists broke laws. . . . Nonconformity, theological and political, has long been a part of the Baptist vocabulary.[2]

Defending the Dissenter

Out of our history of dissent, Baptists have historically defended the principle of the right of dissent. We have upheld the right of the individual to speak his or her mind. Even when we didn't agree with people and their views, we've said each person has every right to express them.

Most of us remember the saying first attributed to the French skeptic, Voltaire: "I may disapprove of what you say, but I will defend to the death your right to say it."[3] Though Baptists wouldn't agree with most of what Voltaire said, historic Baptists would say "Amen" to this sentiment.

In *Our Baptist Story*, Pope Duncan said it this way,

> Toleration was not enough. They (Baptists) insisted on freedom, not toleration. Rather than merely the concession of the right to exist, religious liberty involves also the right to express one's views in public through any and all means of communication. It involves one's right to proclaim his views freely in order to persuade others to embrace them.[4]

Expressing views, and giving others the right to do so, means a willingness to accept dissenting opinions.

A Minority People

Baptists have defended the right of dissent for two key reasons. First, we've upheld it because *we were born as a minority people*. We were the few arrayed against the many. We were the flea on the elephant's back. We were the Chinese dissident facing the tank. As the flea, we sought to protect the powerless, to insure the rights of the weak, to hear the voice of the minority.

Ironically, as we've grown—numerically, financially, and politically—we've begun to muzzle the dissenter in our midst. Now that we're the top dog, now that we're the elephant, we want to still the voices of those who challenge us to remain true to our heritage.

In a recent interview, the much-heard American Baptist speaker and author, Tony Campolo, spoke of the issues facing Southern Baptists. He said,

> The basic problem is that your people have gotten too rich. You have bought into the middle class culture. . . . You can be theologically orthodox, . . . but if you're not calling people to be rebellious against their culture, then you don't have Biblical Christianity.[5]

I don't hear many Baptists today calling for anyone to "rebel" against their culture. Instead, I hear an ominous quiet. We now look on the dissenters—against church, government, or denominational status quo—as unwanted heretics and traitors.

When Baptists were weak babes, they defended the rights of weak babes. Now that we're strong house-owners, we want the babes to stay quiet in the church and in the country.

Baptists today face the question—can we remain truly Baptists and live as a cultural majority group? Though we may not be a majority in number, we've grown to the point that our people and our leaders participate at the highest levels of national life. Breathing such heady air of power can cause us to forget the minority who may find themselves in opposition to it.

A Scriptural People

Baptists have defended the right of dissent, second, because *we've thrived as a scriptural people.*

Though we tend to forget it, God works more in dissenters than in the defenders of the status quo. Recall for a second the way God has revealed himself to us. More often than not, God works in the voice of the one than in the voice of the many.

Of all the Old Testament heroes, none demonstrates this more completely than Elijah. We look in on him in 1 Kings 18. You know the story. Elijah stood as one lonely man of God against 450 of Ahab's hired prophets and 400 more false leaders of Asherah. The people of Israel gathered on Mount Carmel to witness the spectacle.

Elijah set up the contest—his God, Yahweh, against Baal. The one who could call down fire and set the wood aflame to consume the sacrificial bulls would prove the power of his God.

The false prophets called on their God. No answer. They called as the sun walked across the sky. No response. They grew hoarse from their calling, but their words failed. Their god failed. No fire fell.

Then Elijah stepped to the front. He commanded the people to soak the altar with water. They did—three times—and the water filled the gullies. Then Elijah prayed. And the fire fell.

What a picture of dissent against the majority! What an example of dissent against the status quo. God spoke through one minority voice.

God worked in a similar way through Jesus. The majority party shouted, "Crucify him." The majority party arrested him in the dead of night and tried him behind closed doors and sentenced him to an unjust death. The majority party walked past the cross and wagged their fingers at Jesus and said sarcastically, "If you're the Christ, save yourself." The majority party finished the executioner's gruesome work, then wiped their hands of the Nazarene and assumed they were done with him. But, God had other ideas. God worked in the one to say, "Forgive them." God worked in the one to say, "Be not afraid." God worked in the one to proclaim good news, to bestow glad grace, and to offer eternal life.

Baptists have believed in the right and have fought for the right of dissent because we believe *one plus God equals a majority.*

An Insistence on Silence

Sadly, we Baptists find ourselves in peril of giving up the right of dissent within our own fellowship. We see our insistence on silence on numerous fronts. We see it when a Baptist Sunday School Board employee gets demoted because he dared share his opinion about events in the Southern Baptist Convention. We see it when state Baptist newspaper editors and Baptist Press personnel receive pressure to tone down their editorials or they get fired outright for publishing the news as they see it. We see the drive to kill dissent when a book commissioned by the Baptist Sunday School Board gets pulled because it doesn't fit the views of the trustees of that agency. We see it when people of any theological persuasion, right or left, speak out in dissent against the status quo, then receive censure for their viewpoints.

Historically, Baptists believed in the right of expression from the theological left or the theological right. In times past, dissenters were our heroes. Now, however, we look upon the dissenter as an outcast, and we treat the person like a leper.

Allegiance to Majority Rule

We make this mistake for two flawed reasons. First, we reject the dissenter out of a *misapplied allegiance to the principle of majority rule.*

Baptists have lived as a congregational body. This means we give our people the information they need to make a decision. Then, we give them the right to express openly their viewpoints in a church or denominational forum. After open debate, we prayerfully choose a direction, and we vote our conscience. The congregational system has served us well. The majority makes the decision for the body. That's Baptist, and that's good.

But, at the same time the majority ruled, Baptists *have* believed the minority still had the right to be heard and to stay involved. Majority rule has never meant minority exclusion in Baptist life until the last 15 years. Baptists historically said the minority had the right to remain involved in the process. We did this for a very practical reason. We knew we couldn't get along without the minority among us. We also did it because we recognized the minority might have a word or a gift we needed to hear and to share. We certainly recognize this in the local church situation.

What would happen, for example, in your local church if you elected a new pastor with 55 percent of the vote? (We know that wouldn't happen, since most Baptist churches require at least 75 percent.) But, in our scenario, the majority rules and this pastor comes to serve in your congregation.

Then, suppose the new pastor has the singular power, given by the church' constitution and by-laws, to name the nominating committee. In naming the nominating committee, the pastor selects only people who voted for him. He also requires all of them to believe like he believes about a long list of theological, political, and social issues. Then, he makes the nominating committee fill the other committees of the church with people who also voted for him and who also believe the same way about the same list of issues.

Next, this pastor, who serves as the moderator of the church business meeting, (they hold only one per year) uses the position of the chair to stifle discussion from any who might dissent and to control the items that come before the church.

In the sermons and the teaching of this new pastor, the 45% are told their points of disagreement with him make their Christian experience and commitment to the Bible suspect.

The 45 percent who voted against this pastor and don't agree with him on every point of doctrine, social issue, and political position, can no longer serve in positions within the church. They are allowed little, if any, opportunity to express their concerns. Yet, the pastor expects them to tithe, in spite of the fact that many of the 55 percent who control the church give much less than the dissenters to the work of the church.

What do you think would happen to that local church? What would the 45 percent do? What would you do if you were in that 45 percent?

You know what would happen. Either the 45 percent would stop giving or they would find another fellowship. So, to maintain our fellowship, we have sought to live by majority rule but also by minority representation. To do otherwise invites turmoil and schism.

As we well know in recent years, a group known as fundamental-conservatives has consistently won the presidency of the Southern Baptist Convention.

Taking this vote as a mandate, the fundamental-conservative presidents have then stacked the Committee on Committees with people who will follow their direction about who to name to the other committees of the convention. That's their right and the right of the majority.

The difficulty arises because the 45 percent who voted otherwise are shut out of the process and allowed little if any positions of involvement, leadership or voice. In effect, majority rule has come to mean minority exclusion. Though the secular political arena has always worked this way, Baptists traditionally have not.

When any individual or group shuts off and shuts out the minority, we violate Baptist principle! And that cuts across all theological lines. Whether you see yourself as a theological fundamentalist, liberal, conservative or moderate doesn't matter. If you're a Baptist you have the right to dissent against the majority view. And your dissent shouldn't mean exclusion.

Allegiance to Institutional Faith

We tend to deny or dislike the right of dissent in Southern Baptist life today, second, because of a *misplaced allegiance to an institutionalized faith*. In our early history, many fought and some died for the right to believe and practice what they wanted. These dissenters weren't concerned about institutional survival. They were concerned about personal belief.

In the twentieth century, Baptists built monolithic institutions and denominational structures in the effort to spread the word of Christ. We meant well, and our institutions served us ably. Unfortunately, over the years, we have tended to equate zealous Christianity with institutional loyalty. If you gave a high percentage of money to the institutional life of the Southern Baptist Convention, through the Cooperative Program, you and your church were accepted as spiritually correct and denominationally supportive. To dare speak out against institutional structures, methods, or persons meant radicalism of the worst stripe.

Whether one wore the label fundamentalist, liberal, or moderate didn't matter. Denominational loyalty did. So, the right of dissent suffered.

When we shut down dissent—from the right or the left—because it questions a denominational structure, we're confusing our faith with the system. At times, the most loyal thing we can do is to speak out against the sin that makes all institutions, even Southern Baptist ones, deserving of our critique.

The Value of Dissent

Though none of us wants to admit it, Southern Baptists built a system that became an idol for many. We equated the gospel of Christ and the kingdom of God with the structure of our convention. We forgot how to separate them. When persons dissented, we labeled them heretic, losing sight of the fact that dissent against a structure didn't at all mean an equal dissent against God. God loves dissenters! The Bible proves it over and over.

Noah dissented against his neighbors; Moses dissented against Pharaoh; Elijah against Ahab; Amos against false priests; John the Baptist against false religion; Stephen and Peter and John and scads of others against the Pharisees; Jesus against all structures that slay the spirit and rob the soul. Dissent against structures often meant God was at work. Baptists need to remember this.

In the sixteenth century, a young priest searched for a pure religion. He struggled to find his way to God. He poured himself into the life of the institutional faith, hoping to reach harmony with Jesus. But, he found no peace. In fact, he found himself at odds with his church. He rejected the selling of faith and the rigid order that created no salvation. Out of desperation, he turned to the scriptures and discovered again the truth of the gospel, "salvation by grace alone." He nailed his views to the door of the structure at Wittenburg and walked away. Church leaders branded him rebel, heretic, infidel. Martin Luther said, "Here I stand, I can do no other." He lived as a dissenter. Aren't we glad he did?

Notes

[1]For a quick review of Baptist origins, see Robert A. Baker, *The Baptist March in History* (Nashville: Convention Press, 1958) 41–61.

[2]Walter B. Shurden, *Not a Silent People*, (Nashville: Broadman Press, 1972) 16.

[3]Cited from Lewis C. Henry, ed., *Five Thousand Quotations For All Occasions* (Garden City, New York: Doubleday and Company, Inc., 1945) 265.

[4]Pope Duncan, *Our Baptist Story*, (Nashville: Convention Press, 1958) 10.

[5]Cited from *The Word and Way*, 13 February 1992, 13.

Chapter Eight

A Crown or a Towel: Servant Leadership

Matthew 20: 25–26

Almost a Boss

I've always wanted my children to get old enough for me to use their youthful words as fodder for illustrations. Well, mine have now reached that age. Recently, I asked my seven-year old, Andrea: "What's it like when you see Daddy preaching in church?" She thought a moment, then said: "It's almost like I don't have a Daddy." That took me back f or a second. I asked her another question in an attempt to understand her answer. I said: "If it's like you don't have a Daddy, then what do you have?" She said: "It's almost like I have a Boss." I want you to know I stopped asking questions right then! But, I didn't stop thinking about her answer.

I 've struggled with her words ever since, trying to figure out what she meant. On the positive side, she could be telling me I preach "as one with authority," as one whose words deserve attention. On the negative side, she could be telling me I preach like an authoritarian, as if I'm *demanding* attention to my words.

I think my struggle sums up the dilemma we all face. How do we who serve as leaders within the body of Christ (both clergy and laity) gain authority without falling into authoritarianism? How do we get people to listen to us, to respond to us, and to follow us without *demanding* that they do so?

Persuasion or Domination

Without getting too deeply into the whole issue of leadership styles, we can say that leaders typically follow one of two methods. They lead by the art of "persuasion" or they lead by the art of "domination."

The one who leads by persuasion seeks to win friends and influence people through the power of caring relationships. This person develops followers through a team concept of work. He or she discovers authority as it is won through gentle service and mutual respect for other persons.

Traditionally, Baptists have accepted the "persuasive "style of leadership in all its ramifications. We have believed that no distinction exists between the clergy and the laity; that everyone in the church has an equal voice and an equal vote; that every task in the vineyard, no matter how visible or invisible, is equal in importance to God; that every individual, whether pastor in the pulpit or kitchen worker in the pew, gains authority not by virtue of office, but by virtue of faithfulness in ministry to brothers and sisters in Christ.

The Transcendent Leader

Our traditional Baptist principle of leadership, however, finds itself losing big chunks of ground today to the armies of those who champion the "domination" method of leadership.

The "domination" style of leadership expects people to follow because a person holds a particular office or position. It wields influence because of what it can do either to reward or punish other persons. The dominator works independently, telling subordinates what to do after he or she has decided it for themselves. This leader expects total acquiescence from others in matters of opinion and method.

Unfortunately, the dominator style has set up camp among Baptists, and scores of Baptists find themselves responding favorably to the coat of arms on the general's tent.

Without belaboring old news, listen for a moment to the sounds of our modern interpreters of what it means to be a Baptist leader.

The new Baptist leaders demand adherence to their authority. They say: "Obey your rulers and submit to them."

The new Baptist leaders demand agreement with their theology. They say: "If we say that pickles have souls then they better teach that pickles have souls."

The new Baptist leaders demand acceptance of their ecclesiology. They say: "A laity led church will be a weak church anywhere on God's earth."

These words and others like them bring to mind an image of a transcendent leader, standing high above his (I choose the masculine gender deliberately) people, delivering to them the omnipotent word, which the people dare not question. He lives a life removed—from the normal struggles of life. He lives on a pedestal lifted up above others.

Saddaam Hussein Style

During the Persian Gulf War, we learned more about Saddam Hussein than we ever wanted to know. One article described his war-time home. Hussein lived secluded in a German-built, sixty-five-million dollar bunker. The bunker housed incredible luxuries for a man at war. We saw him emerge periodically to make pronouncements to his people. He used strong God-language to affirm the faithful, to intimidate his enemies, and to maintain his own power. Then he disappeared again, accepting none of the ambiguities and hardships his people suffered.

Watching Hussein, I thought of the authoritarian leadership style that seems so prevalent among us. The person lives a secluded life, separated from people, emerging only on Sunday to use vivid God-talk, to proclaim the word of the Lord and dare anyone to dispute it. His words assure him of his power and he disappears again, off to another conference, to share with another group his infallible truth.

Recently, a member of the pulpit committee of a prominent church told me of talking with a minister they were considering. In the interview the prospective pastor said: "I will do no funerals; I will conduct no weddings; I will not do hospital visitation; and I'll have no time for counseling." I wondered, as I heard this, "Where did that man learn his concept of ministry?" Certainly not from scripture, and certainly not from historic Baptists!

Origins of the Dominator

Watching this transcendent style at work, I cannot help but wonder how it became the dominant view among Baptists. (And, if the last decade of Baptist history tells us anything, it tells us this is now the dominant view). We could blame it on the CEO mentality that has invaded the church. This outlook sees the pastor as the executive of the corporation and expects him to operate this way. We could blame it on the "personality types" who enter the ministry or serve as lay leaders in the church. These persons, looking for a place to gratify their personal needs for self-esteem gravitate to structures, like the church, that depend on volunteers for lay ministry and for people to accept a "call" to clergy tasks. I suspect, however, the explanation goes even deeper than either of these. The "domination style" or the "transcendent style" of leadership now threatens to dominate our Southern Baptist family for two basic reasons.

The Crown Bestowers

First, we find ourselves dominated by the "transcendent" style of leadership because the **people we call Baptists decided to embrace** it **and to reject the servant way Jesus chose.**

When the Southern Baptist Convention passed the infamous Resolution Number Five in San Antonio in 1988, it knocked the concept of the priesthood of the believer off the pedestal of Baptist theology. Simultaneously, it put a pedestal under the concept of authoritarian leadership in Baptist polity.

Tragically, laypeople played the major role in both jobs. Preachers could never become anything but servant leaders unless their people allowed it or demanded it to happen.

In 1 Samuel 8:5-22, we find an interesting episode in the life of the prophet Samuel. Samuel is old. The people of Israel fear for the future. They want comfort and assurance, certainty and guidance. So, they demand of Samuel, "Appoint for us a king to govern us like all the nations." Samuel warns them of the dangers of having a king. A king will demand loyalty; a king will brook no dissent; a king will send you places you don't want to go; a king will claim absolute control.

The scripture says:

> This is what the king who will reign over you will do: He will take your sons and make them serve with his chariots and horses, and they will run in front of his chariots. Some he will assign to be commanders of thousands and commanders of fifties, and others to plow his ground and reap his harvest, and still others to make weapons of war and equipment for his chariots. He will take your daughters to be perfumers and cooks and bakers. He will take the best of your fields and vineyards and olive groves and give it to his officials and attendants. Your menservants and maidservants and the best of your cattle and donkeys he will take for his own use. He will take a tenth of your flocks, and you yourselves will become his slaves. When that day comes, you will cry out for relief from the king you have chosen, and the Lord will not answer you in that day.

In spite of the warnings of Samuel, the people persisted. They said, "We want a king over us. " So, they anointed a king. His name was Saul and he fell in love with his crown. He fell so in love with it that he tried to kill his son, Jonathan, and his former friend, David, in order to keep it perched on his head.

The people wanted a king. Nothing much has changed. Scores of Baptist people want a king. They want someone to make salvation simple, someone to make ambiguities clear, someone to make gray issues black and white, someone to give them an anchor of certainty in the midst of an ocean of flux. The demand of the people for a king creates a domination style of leadership.

The Crown Seekers

This "domination style" of ministry threatens the principle of servant-leadership, second, because **crown-bestowers never have to look far to find crown-seekers.**

Apparently, it has always been this way. People can always find someone willing to wear a crown.

Even the original twelve disciples found themselves playing the "Domination Game" from time to time. The Gospels record their dispute about who would be greatest, who would be the chief, who would lead, who would wear the crowns in the kingdom of God (Matt 18:1; 20:20–28; Mark 9:33–35).

Crown-bestowers and crown-seekers always live among us, among those called fundamentalist Baptists *and* among those called moderate Baptists. We'll never suffer from a lack of people who want the seat at the head of the table. We'll always find someone who wants to sit in the councils of power and lord it over lesser persons.

No one of us owns a special immunity to this particular spiritual temptation. Let us admit that our theory of servant leadership often outruns our reality.

The Jesus Model

Thankfully, though, for everyone who seeks to live out the persuasive model of leadership, Jesus gives us the divine example of the alternative method. Though both Satan and the people of Israel offered him a crown, Jesus refused to walk that transcendent road.

Instead, Jesus chose the path of incarnational ministry. He accepted stripes so we can experience healing. He felt the power draining out of him so it could flow into us. He emptied himself and lived among us so we can fill ourselves with his presence and live with him. He lived as a "persuader," not as a "dominator." He found his authority not because he demanded it, but because he earned it by sacrificial living.

In Matthew 20:25-26, Jesus offers us the divine pattern to gain authority. His words were born out of a context of self-seeking. The mother of James and John had requested, as mothers are tempted to do, special privilege for her boys. Jesus refused to acknowledge the request as legitimate.

The other disciples learned of the mother's efforts and reacted with anger toward James and John. At this point, Jesus delivered his assessment of the divine method of authority. He said,

> You know that the rulers of the Gentiles lord it over them, and their great men exercise authority over them. It shall not be so among you; but whoever would be great among you must be your servant, and whoever would be first among you must be your slave.

I don't know what these words say to you. They tell me two things. First, they say the Lord's way of leadership contradicts the typical human style. People of faith shouldn't seek to project themselves forward as the "Gentiles" do. Second, these words tell me God evaluates greatness on an upside-down scale. God looks not to success on the world's terms, but to servanthood in his kingdom. When one person ministers to another, that person unleashes greatness.

As a boy growing up in Greenwood, South Carolina, I read the story of Joseph de Veuster, a Belgian priest who, at the age of 33, went to serve as a missionary on the Hawaiian Island of Molokai. Father de Veuster served for 16 years on that island among the leper colony, enduring the filth and the stench of the dreaded Leper island. After eight years, he contracted leprosy himself.

Many, including family, friends and church superiors, urged him to leave the colony and to return home so he could live out his last days in comfort. Father Damien, as he was called, said to all of them, "I would refuse to be cured if my departure from the island and abandoning all my work here were to be the price." Eight years later, he died, still serving "his lepers."

Even as a boy, not yet a Christian, I remember thinking: "de Veuster was a great man." Incarnational servants always are. Transcendent lords never can be.

Jesus shows us servant leadership as we've historically understood it. He calls us to put away our desire for a crown today and pick up the desire for a towel. He encourages us to trade in our front seats in the White House for the back seats of some buses. Jesus asks us to step down off our pedestals and walk into the muddy streets. He leads us to incarnate the gospel for people, rather than to inflict the gospel upon people.

To Serve in Hell

In John Milton's *Paradise Lost*, we hear the voice of Satan say, "Better to reign in hell than to serve in heaven."[1]

I think Jesus would have us rephrase that comment today. Jesus would have us say, "Better to serve in hell than to reign in heaven."

That's Jesus' style of leadership. He gave up the reign of heaven to serve in the hell of this sinful age. That's the incarnational style. That's the historic Baptist style. Our principle calls us to re-capture and re-assert the Jesus way--that authority arises out of service and that power arises out of weakness.

Notes

[1]Cited in John Bartlett, *Familiar Quotations* (Boston: Brown and Little, 1938) 148.

Chapter Nine

Vive le Différence:
Unity Within Diversity

Psalm 133:1

An Impossible Question

Recently, a newspaper reporter called and asked me this question: "What does your church believe about the validity of a living will?" You need to know before I tell you how I answered him, I live in a town almost equally divided between Catholics and Baptists. So, when the paper carries an article dealing with current topics, the writer makes sure to get a Catholic and a Protestant (usually a Baptist response). I'm certain the reporter had already called, or soon would call, the diocese to get the Catholic view of the issue. Now, though, he had called me.

After a few moments of reflection, I responded something like this:

> I really cannot say what my "church" believes because I can speak only for myself. We definitely believe in the sanctity of life, but no Baptist preacher can speak for the beliefs of all of his people on such an issue as this.

I noticed the newspaper article that followed said nothing about my response. And I was not surprised. My response, however, revealed a truth about Baptists that I learned early. I couldn't give a "Baptist" position because our people reach their own decisions, and we have little or no full agreement on most issues. Someone said once, "If you get three Baptists in the same room, you'll end up with three opinions (or maybe four because one will change his or her mind within a few moments).

Baptists aren't this way just because they're cantankerous (although some of us Baptists certainly are that). Instead, Baptists are this way because of a long-standing principle that we have embraced. This principle, called "unity within diversity," gives all Baptists the right to reach their own conclusions about the Bible and how it relates to their Christian faith.

A Biblical Ideal

In Psalm 133:1, we hear these beautiful words, "Behold, how good and pleasant it is for the brethren to dwell together in unity." All of us would heartily concur with the conclusion of this psalmist. It is "good," and it is "beautiful" for the "brethren to dwell together in unity." We pray often and face the challenge daily to live together in the unity of the bonds of faith.

The questions, however, that this text bring to us are: "Where do we find our source of unity? In the midst of our diversity, how can we discover actual unity?"

If we were not diverse, we would have no problem with unity. But, all of us can see and realize our diversity. We live with diversity within the body of faith called the local church and within the body of faith called the Southern Baptist Convention. This is the way it has always been.

In his book, *Baptists: The Passionate People*, Burtt Potter, Jr., writes, "The diversity of Baptist people has been obvious from their beginnings. They've differed over missions, the origin of the denomination, interpretation of the Scriptures and in their ordinances."[1]

A diversity of educational levels, economic statuses, theological outlooks, political persuasions, and physical attributes characterizes us as Southern Baptists. In fact, it characterizes us as human beings.

If I wanted, I could ask a series of theological questions that would eventually lead all of us to a point of complete disunity. For instance, I could ask: "How many of you accepted Christ dramatically, following years of painful rebellion and rejection of God? How many became Christians as youngsters, growing up in Christian homes and into the faith naturally, without great drama? How many are strict Calvinists, who believe that everything that happens to you occurs from the direct will of God? How many are Arminian, who believe God allows us multiples of choices and that within those choices we determine much of what actually happens to us? How many don't know exactly which you are? How many of you believe women should share equal opportunities as men in the leadership and service of the church and how many don't? How many believe in the pretribulation rapture of the church and how many don't believe in a rapture at all? How many don't have any idea what either of these mean? How many believe God created the world in six literal days and how many believe the six days represent long epochs of time in which God performed his creative work? How many believe in the plenary verbal theory of the inspiration of the Bible and how many accept the dynamic theory (and again, how many have no idea what either of these two mean)? I could continue with the list, but I hope we all see the point I'm trying to make.

Baptists live within diversity. We cannot help it because we are people marked by different histories, different educations, different frameworks from which to see the world.

Dr. Bill Leonard, head of the department of Christianity at Samford University, spoke recently of the difficulties within the Southern Baptist Convention and said,

> Until the current denominational controversy, the SBC stated its doctrines in terms broad enough to include churches which reflected a wide variety of diverse theological traditions. . . . Framers of the denomination's confessional statements recognized the SBC's diversity and resisted efforts to define dogma too narrowly lest they alienate large segments of the constituency.[2]

Southern Baptists have historically shown a willingness to embrace their theological diversity as a strength rather than to see it as a weakness. Whether we will admit it or not, our founding documents as a convention state we came together out of a desire to do missions together rather than out of any uniform doctrinal stance.

The opening paragraph of the constitution of the Southern Baptist Convention says our purpose in coming together was to provide "a plan for eliciting, combining and directing the energies of the denomination for the propagation of the gospel."[3] Nothing in our founding documents says anything about a doctrinal agreement as necessary or beneficial for our unity. To put it in a sentence, we exist as a convention, and as a local church, because of a *functional* purpose—to do the work of Christ—not out of the *doctrinal* purpose—to make sure everyone believes the same thing.

A Revision of History

In the last few years, however, our new leadership has begun to try to re-write our history. They now want us to believe we must find doctrinal uniformity in order to continue functional ministry. They insist we came together over doctrinal unity, rather than over missions objectives. Yet, our founding constitution says nothing about doctrinal conformity. The problem that has occurred in the last twelve years has occurred because of a lack of respect for the Baptist hallmark of "unity within diversity."

Let me give one example of this new thought. It comes from Reverend Adrian Rodgers, three-time president of the Southern Baptist Convention within the last thirteen years, and the unquestioned pastoral leader of our new convention. In his 1987 presidential address, Rodgers said, "The basis of our unity is not missions and evangelism. The basis of our unity is spiritual and doctrinal. We do what we do because we are what we are."[4]

Now, with all due respect to Reverend Rodgers, this understanding is a total revision of our founding documents and our Baptist history. We *did* come together over missions and evangelism! Remember the purpose statement of the original constitution. We organized for the purpose of "directing the energies of the denomination for the propagation of the gospel." That says nothing about coming together out of a uniformity of doctrine. We were diverse in our doctrines from the very beginning.

But, the current leadership in the Southern Baptist Convention wants to change all of that. They do not like our diversity.

As Leonard puts it, "Intricate doctrinal definitions have become more important to many Southern Baptists as a source of denominational unity," and the "cultural and denominational ties that once held the SBC together have collapsed."[5]

We can trace much of our present dilemma directly to a lack of willingness to allow for the broad range of diversity that Baptists traditionally held. When the new leadership insists on doctrinal uniformity in all those who serve on our trustee boards, when they insist on creedal adherence in all those who get hired in our seminaries and other Southern Baptist Convention institutions, when they call all the others everything from liberals to skunks to bureaucratic buzzards (to name just a few of the more colorful titles they have hung on those who disagree with them), our new leadership shows their dislike for our diversity.

A Basis of Faith

I realize whenever we use the word "diversity" someone will ask: "Does that mean we can believe anything we want and still be a Christian and a Baptist?"

No, of course it doesn't mean that. But, it does mean that outside of a basic, irreducible minimum, we do not set doctrinal barriers on the lives of our people. The key, of course, is to define that basic, irreducible minimum. What does every Christian have to believe in order to wear the name of Christ? For me—and I can only speak for myself—the irreducible minimum centers around the person and work of Jesus Christ. It can be summed up by referring to Romans 10:9.

While a boy in Greenwood, South Carolina, I recall an elderly gentleman, with a derby hat on his head, a pair of wire-framed glasses on his nose, a flannel shirt draped on his shoulders, and a Bible in his hands. He testified one morning in church and said: "How do I know that Jesus is mine? 'Cause I believe Romans 10:9." I've never forgotten those words.

"If you confess with your mouth that Jesus Christ is Lord and believe in your hearts that God has raised him from the dead, thou shalt be saved."

That was good for Paul and Silas, and that's good enough for me. You can add any doctrine you want around that, but none of the additional doctrine makes me a Christian or a Baptist. The inward experience (belief in the heart) and the outward confession (confess with your mouth) usher me into the present and eternal presence of almighty God.

The irreducible minimum of our faith centers around Jesus Christ. What we believe about Jesus Christ and how we live our lives out of our commitment to Christ determine the validity of our faith. This alone take us to the throne of grace.

Anything and everything that doesn't center around Jesus Christ is really non-essential for salvation. We spend so much time debating the other issues, and that's fine, but these other issues don't save a person. Gentiles in the day of Paul never worried about "how" the Bible was inspired because they didn't know what a Bible was. That's not to minimize the value of the Bible, but let's be honest about what's essential for salvation and fellowship within our Baptist body. Until the last 150 years, very few people had ever read a Bible. And, even today, millions of people come to Christ in third-world countries and do so without benefit of a Bible.

Our battle over the Bible—whether we'll describe it by using the word inerrant, or infallible, or fully inspired, or totally trustworthy, or whatever term you want to put on it—really does nothing to advance the kingdom of God. And, it does everything to harm the unity of our diverse people.

I don't remember where I heard it first, but an old story illustrates my point. One day, Jesus healed two blind men. Quite by chance, they met each other on the street on the afternoon of their healing. They shared together the miraculous gift of sight.

The taller of the two men asked, "How did Jesus heal you?" The second one answered. "Jesus picked up a little dirt off the ground. He put it in the palm of his hand and then spat into it. He rubbed the spittle into the dirt, rubbed it over my eyes and instantly, I could see."

The tall man's face grew red as the other one talked. When he finished, the taller man fumed, "Surely, he didn't do it as you've described. Jesus healed me with two words. He said, 'Be healed,' and my eyes were opened. I'm sure he always heals the same way."

The two men fell into an intense argument and soon became so angry they lost their tempers and almost came to blows. In a huff, they turned away from each other and went their separate ways.

And, so began the first two denominations—the Mudites and the anti-Mudites! Instead of celebrating the common healing they had received and the vision they both shared, the two men fought over the method of the cure.

In his sermon of 1987 at the Baptist General Convention of Texas, Paul Powell, then the President of the Texas Baptist Convention, said:

> We must remember that it is not necessary for two people to agree on everything in order to work together. We don't have to see eye-to-eye to walk arm-in-arm. Two men (people) can be brothers (and sisters) without being identical twins. We can disagree without being disagreeable. We should not fear holding differing opinions as long as we do not have an unbrotherly attitude.[6]

I like those words. We have all kinds in our fellowship of Baptists. Diversity is a hallmark of ours—and I think a strength. Let us not fight over our differences, but let us unite over our common desire to see our communities and our world come to know the love and the grace of Jesus Christ, our Lord.

Most of you know the phrase, first spoken by John Amos Comenius, a seventeenth-century Moravian leader. He exhorted, "In essentials unity; in non-essentials, liberty; in all things, charity."[7]

It's not always easy to determine the essentials and the non-essentials, but let's keep centered on Jesus Christ. And, it's not easy to practice charity in all things. But, let's seek to do so in the power of God's Holy Spirit. If we can do that as an individual, as churches, as state conventions, and as a national body, we can find our way out of our painful and tragic cross fire. God grant us wisdom to live together in unity, in the midst of our diversity.

Notes

[1]Potter, *Baptists: The Passionate People* (Nashville: Broadman Press, 1973) 62.

[2]Cited from a message preached at The Southern Baptist Theological Seminary during "Denominational Heritage Week."

[3]Potter, 58.

[4]Quoted in the *Word and Way*, 25 June 1987, 3.

[5]Cited from a sermon at The Southern Baptist Theological Seminary during "Denominational Heritage Week."

[6]Sermon preached at the annual meeting of the Baptist General Convention of Texas in November of 1987.

[7]Cited in *International Thesaury of Quotations*, 118.